NEW ENGLAND RETURNS TO THE WHITE HOUSE

"How Back Bay in Boston scorned it all. . . . It was as though Coolidge was the reincarnated Puritan, the poor relation of Back Bay, forever appearing to mock and humiliate it."

(Page 88)

CALVIN COOLIDGE

THE MAN WHO IS PRESIDENT

BY

WILLIAM ALLEN WHITE

New York
THE MACMILLAN COMPANY
1925

Mr 26 1926

6
· C7773W5c

178095

TABLE OF CONTENTS

PART I
"BLESSED ARE THE MEEK"

PART II
"FOR THEY SHALL INHERIT THE EARTH"

PART III
CINDERELLA AT A GAY PARTY

LIST OF ILLUSTRATIONS

PART I

BLESSED ARE THE MEEK

CALVIN COOLIDGE

CHAPTER I

IN WHICH WE STATE OUR THESIS

An introduction to this book seems necessary, that the reader may not begin it under a misapprehension. The book is not a formal biography. It is not an attempt to write a history of the quarter of a century during which Calvin Coolidge has been in politics. The biographical material and the history which the book contains are in it only because they help to explain the man whose story shall follow. The book is a study of a personality.

The monstrous magnification which follows the white light that beats upon a throne, makes every President more or less unique. We see him always somewhat out of drawing. Every daily act and his most casual words are isolated by environing events; not thrown into perspective with the rest of his life. Thus any President becomes in the popular conception a superman, in spite of his ordinary character. Yet sometimes men of odd sizes do come to the White House; men of peculiar qualities, men with areas of exceptional powers. In the fifty passing years, the presidency has shown us three such men:

3

Wilson, Roosevelt and Grover Cleveland. Whatever strength and genius Grant had was displayed in the army and not in Washington. Our other Presidents in the half century have been the standard product of our politics—men with the faults and virtues of their craft—not a bad craft as crafts go, however much it is abused.

Calvin Coolidge, although he is the most incorrigible politician that has come to the White House in this generation, strangely enough is the most baffling person who has ruled us in the memory of living man. He is baffling chiefly because he is not candid. His self-reservation is not conscious. He refuses to explain himself; to help the people to judge him, to boast or bluster or justify himself. Perhaps he uses the first personal pronoun as often as his more outspoken predecessors used it; certainly he is no violet by a mossy stone. He esteems himself highly; and why not? But their I's had the portrait painter's camel's hair on one end, and so their I's blocked them into the canvas and finally their I's outlined them in detail as they talked. Coolidge's I is blunt—unilluminating.

The chapters that shall follow in this book are submitted in the endeavor to find the man behind his mask of protective modesty. He hides not so much in fear, as from habit. And when one would ask why he began the habit of reticence and self-concealment, one must go back to his boyhood, back even beyond his boyhood into his ancestry and back

CALVIN COOLIDGE, AGE THREE

"We are cast in iron molds. Heredity pours the plastic personality of infancy into a time and a place. There a personality emerges, a static man is created."

(Page 5)

of that into the environment from which he came
and wherein he found himself as a child. We are
cast in iron molds. Heredity pours the plastic
personality of infancy into a time and a place.
There in a few years a character is formed; a personality emerges, a static man is created. Changing
health only can change the spirit or human substance, or individual equation or whatever you will
call it, that comes out of those inexorable forms
of blood and training. And the spirit of the man
sometimes even gauges the health of his body.

In reviewing the career of Calvin Coolidge, we
find him repeating again and again a certain curve
in his career. The spirit made in him by the biological and social fates, once it was formed, always
has reacted to outside stimuli in one manner. Fortuitous circumstances pass before him, as they file
before every man; he reacts upon those circumstances after the impulse of his heart, the education
of his mind; in short, according to his judgment. In
normal health a man puts a specific amount of
energy into his convictions; the thing we call will.
He puts a definite amount of self-interest into his
actions, a certain degree of altruism into his
judgments. So that any man's career is, at the close
of the period of his normal bodily vigor, a series
of repetitions. Only as his body fails does the
equation change which is represented by his judgment upon the passing circumstances. Even then,
even when cooling blood or hardening arteries alters

his stock of energy, even when his blood and his glands have ceased to function in the accustomed way, even amid "change and decay" the spirit far back in the heart of him, the essence of him that is forever young, where the eternal youth aspires after it can no longer act with judgment, even then and there at the end, whatever is immortal lives. Calvin Coolidge in the White House is only the little boy from Vermont.

Of course some seismic event may transform him. He may go upon a journey where he shall see a "great light" and a Voice may call him "Saul, Saul." Cataclysmic regeneration is not impossible; but it is unusual and generally temporary. So if we would know the man in the White House whom the god Demos has appointed to rule over us—and it is indeed necessary to know him if we use him well— we must see him before the crust of habit covered him, we must realize that we are dealing here with something more than a dapper little man in the high hat of a high office, but a person with a human spirit created divinely by biological and social laws, years and years ago; created indeed out of forces which began culminating generations ago. To lie about him, to belittle him, to sneer at him, to horn him because he is not like the run of the herd will avail nothing. To use him we must know him, allow for his curve of judgment, help him husband his strength, and we must not play upon his obvious weaknesses for our selfish ends.

And here at the threshold of this examination of Calvin Coolidge, the individual, let us repeat for emphasis that this is not a formal biography, nor a biographical history, but a serious consideration of a man whom we shall find simple enough when we know him, and only baffling because he hides himself; a normal, kindly, most human creature—faulty, of course, and indubitably strong, or he would not be President; interesting less for what he is, than for the way he conceals it.   And let us also never forget that here is the instrument which, for the moment, fate must use to work out the day's destiny.

CHAPTER II

THE CHILD AND HIS BACKGROUND

Calvin Coolidge is an enigma, not an accident.

In every career chance enters. But in no career that takes a man gradually to the world's place of greatest power does chance govern. Twenty times has Calvin Coolidge's name gone into the American ballot box. Nineteen times the people have given him their approval. And the twentieth time he was away on his honeymoon and could not make a canvass. Harding stood seven times and lost once; Wilson stood and won three times; Taft won twice and lost once; Roosevelt won six out of eight; McKinley eleven out of fourteen; Cleveland five out of seven; Harrison two out of three, and so back to antiquity. The people are not fooled when they have a chance to test a man time after time. There is no better gauge of a man's capacity for public service than a long series of direct votes of the people. This does not guarantee character entirely, nor ability along many important lines of activity. But surely the people sense a man's worth to them; surely they know their own moods, their own hearts' desires, which change with the years, and surely the

8

men whom our people pick for servants do represent some passing phrase of American aspiration. And when a man has gone into twenty elections and has won nineteen, he has something in him which compels confidence and which represents the popular will.

Now, Calvin Coolidge is an enigma largely because those whom he baffles do not understand him nor the hearts of the people who chose him. For a quarter century American politics has been dominated by men who made some pretense at rugged candor, or of graceful unconcealment of their major plans and minor motives. In that time our Presidents, Cleveland, McKinley, Roosevelt, Taft, Wilson, and Harding, have been men who were obviously ashamed of their reserves. And the people have been anxious in all those years for frankness in public men; because the popular heart has been, on the whole, expansive, unafraid, generous to the point even of justice. As far back as Cleveland's day popular aspiration was not so much for prosperity as for an equitable distribution of the fruits of prosperity.

A tremor came; the gold standard was menaced. McKinley, the least candid of our modern Presidents, was picked in a day of anxiety when the people considered self-preservation ahead of altruism. McKinley passed. Roosevelt came. America was interested in problems of distribution, problems of equitable allotment of the increment of industry and

agriculture rather than in problems of mere accumulation of wealth.

So Roosevelt, the roaring, robust, frank and contentious, went about applying the Golden Rule to
capitalism in a loud tone of voice. President Taft,
representing those who disliked the contentious attitude of popular righteousness, appeared every morning on the front porch of the White House to quarrel
with the United States. Then he faded quickly to
give way to Wilson, who only deepened the Roosevelt tone of voice. He went right on aspiring—
which meant more justice, quicker turnovers and
smaller profits. Harding came—a kindly, candid,
babbling man, who talked plausibly in the front of
the house while the thieves worked in the larders.

Then the people, who rejected Wilson and his
kind, and forgot Roosevelt and his kind, turned
instinctively to Coolidge. He is the apotheosis of
the America of the first half of the third decade of
the twentieth century. Perhaps the picture of the
soul of these timid times may be made by cartooning
the rich man slipping through the dark wilderness
of this world, with one hand on his purse and the
other on his gun, caring little for justice and hoping
chiefly to save his skin.

Coolidge, tried by twenty juries and found honest,
industrious, capable and not so vain of his courage
as to be dangerous, became, by the precise working
of the law of spiritual and political affinities, the
man of the hour. The miracle of it is as inexplicable

as gravitation or the processes of life—and as inexorable.

That is the enigma of Coolidge—not his character, which is fairly simple, nor his luck, which is our indolent word for the ancient process of political selection. The enigma of Coolidge is a crossword puzzle, wherein we must find only the traits of the man and the tendencies of the times that fit the squares.

So let us begin with Silence—find its root cause in Coolidge, and its deep need in leadership. Silent Cal or Cautious Cal, if we must be exact in his pseudonym at home, is a product of New England. His type—taciturn, monosyllabic, crabbed, dry, weaned on a clothespin—probably is no more common in New England than in any other section of America, no more common in other parts of New England than in Vermont, but in New England it is understood better than elsewhere. In Vermont crabbed taciturnity is accounted a virtue. New England was settled by a race that wanted to be let alone. They were a throwback, spiritually, to the men of the Old Testament. They cultivated Old Testament virtues, parsimony in all human relations. A Yankee can skin a Jew. Moses was "slow of speech and of a slow tongue." Coolidge, looking down his nose, seems "as meek as Moses." He isn't. Neither was Moses. So much for New England.

Now for Vermont. Two hundred years ago it was pioneered by hunters and trappers—men who lived by silence! Farming was an incident of their lives, the by-product of the odd moments when the ground was not frozen. A beautiful land is Vermont, a hilly country which passes for mountainous until one knows the Rockies. Here among the rocks and wooded hills grew up five generations of Coolidges, who, not being silent enough themselves, brought out of Connecticut a remote strain of Indian blood.

And here on the Fourth of July, 1872, Calvin Coolidge was born. He grew up a shy, old-fashioned little boy who used to run away and hide when the neighbors came! Said he in recalling those times:

"Most of the visitors would sit in the kitchen with Father and Mother, and the hardest thing in the world for me was to have to go through that kitchen door and greet the visitors. By fighting hard I used to manage to get through that kitchen door. I'm all right now with old friends, but every time I meet a stranger I have to stand by the old kitchen door a minute. It's hard!"

Now, this shy little boy in the Vermont town was no more queer than the average boy. He was husky, wholesome, normal. He did his chores, herded with his kind, fought and wrestled and scratched and lied, and loved and hated his fellows and his elders, lived in the dream world of childhood very much as any boy in any other part of the world. He was silent and freckled; home-made and hand-spanked. The hills and brooks and woods about him became a

THE PLYMOUTH SCHOOL

"He was silent, freckled; home-made and hand-spanked."

(Page 12)

part of the boy, and somewhat because he lived in a little dot of a village in a notch between two hills and had few playmates, except an older sister whom he adored, and certain doting grandparents who adored him, the hereditary tendency to silence deepened in him. It made him awkward rather than visionary and probably gave him a duller exterior than his heart and mind justified.

It is hard for a reader born in the West or born in the city to realize Plymouth, Vermont, where Calvin Coolidge's father was born. President Coolidge's second New Year in the White House found his father, a man in his eighties, celebrating New Year's Eve in the home town. The entire village, thirty-five in number, was gathered in the country store, the only store in Plymouth. For fifty years Father Coolidge had run that store. He sold it a few years ago for $800 to his clerk. In his fifty years as a merchant he has saved something more than $25,000. The whole commerce of Plymouth had trickled through that store in that half century; and profits have been filtered out by the penny—profits on the excess produce of the meager farms going to the world beyond, profits on the few needs of a frugal people for goods coming out of a complicated civilization.

Colonel George Harvey, himself a Vermonter, tells this Coolidge story: When Calvin was five years old he had managed by working for the promoter of a local entertainment to get a ticket of admission but needed some incidental spending money, and asked for it. Freely and generously he got a silver three-cent piece from his father—wealth beyond the dreams of avarice. But shortly before the day of the performance his father called the boy to him and said, "Now, son, we are liable to get into hard times, and I need that three-cent piece. We mustn't spend it. We must save every penny. For if the election goes wrong and General Hancock wins, we're going to have hard times."

The boy gave up the silver piece; the election passed. General Garfield won. The father came around, returned the identical three-cent piece, saying,

"Now don't spend it all foolishly."

And youth had its fling! And here we create the second word needed in the crossword puzzle, "Economy!"

The Coolidges were prosperous people—people of consequence, in Plymouth. Grandfather Coolidge had inherited something like $10,000 from his father, who in his turn was a man of parts (a public servant also) on an inheritance of probably $5,000. And when the fitful fever of his presidential term shall close, even if Calvin Coolidge spends every penny of his princely salary, he can retire to Plymouth upon his patrimony, a man of large means. This is Vermont. Its politics is honest because statecraft is chiefly concerned with schools and roads; and every penny that comes into the state treasury is

PLYMOUTH, VERMONT

"It is hard for a reader born in the city to realize Plymouth, Vermont, where Coolidge was born."

(Page 13)

marked and numbered so that it would be impossible to steal it. No Vermonter has ever been daring enough to enter a career of corruption on those numbered pennies. Honesty in Vermont is not merely the best policy. It is a necessary virtue from which there is no alternative.

And Calvin Coolidge, son of the village squire who was also the constable of forty years' standing, also sometimes deputy sheriff, and occasionally member of the state legislature in one house or another, a merchant prince and a bank director in Ludlow, the village in the valley; Calvin Coolidge, the pampered son of the calif of Plymouth, split his wood, worked his garden, curried his horse, milked his cow, slopped his pig, and fed his chickens, as became the scion of a noble house in those latitudes.

Life pressed in upon the silent boy its varied experiences. To him came early the knowledge of death. His grandfather, who had been the boy's idol, went first, and when the awe of that death had faded somewhat from the child's heart, his mother went. It must have cut a deep gash that left a never-healing scar in his heart—that death of his mother —and then his sister, who had been his playmate through the years of his childhood and early youth, was called. The little graveyard near the country store where he was born holds much that was dear to him. So, because he was silent, because he was inarticulate, he grew spiritually a bit gawky, and never recovered the nice social poise that makes one easy in the presence of his fellows. Coolidge was always a Cal as boy and man. Your Yankee nicknames every one to keep him humble, allowing no neighbor to heroize himself. Even though he was repressed, and though in play the other boys and girls sensed his isolation, yet they knew it was not the isolation of pride nor the aloofness of a dull mind. He took his place and did his part in a boy world; went through his school course in the solid old stone schoolhouse at Plymouth with no distinction, good or bad. We see him in a picture standing before the schoolhouse door, in no way distinguished from the other little boys and girls in home-made clothes and with home-made hearts. A shy country boy, aged twelve, he went into the valley to the academy at Ludlow, with his elder sister. But he went as a squire's son and a somebody. Not many boys from Plymouth could go to the Ludlow Academy. Always the Coolidges were landowners—aristocrats. Mark that. It is significant.

At the academy he did the day's work, went from childhood into adolescence, played the game, mingled with boys and girls of his age, and tradition in the village says that Nature took her course with him, and that in his later teens he fell gently but insecurely in love, and backed out again, after the manner of his kind. He made few friends and held them fast and loved them dearly and never forgot them; read few books and knew them well—

COOLIDGE'S LUDLOW ACADEMY CLASS PICTURE

"In the class picture his face shows a quiet, contented, strong youth, born of the ruling classes, sure of himself without conceit."

(Page 17)

old-fashioned, center-table books: Shakespeare and
the Bible; Bunyan, and standard eighteenth-century
authors, and the Red Line poets of a later day and
generation.   He was as normal and hardy, undis-
tinguished and American, as a red apple.   But also
he was New England.

The Coolidges never went West.   The daring
bred of boundless hope and inextinguishable faith
in the plans of God and the capacity of men to
follow and fathom those plans, was not implanted
in the boy's heart.   He was born and bred in the
land of caution.   His anchor was grounded in common sense.   The uncommon sense of the adventurer,
the pioneer, the crusader, had no place in his heart.
He was graduated from Ludlow Academy, went to
college, and has lived all his life within a hundred
miles of it!   All his other academy classmates have
gone.   In the class picture his face shows a quiet,
contented, strong youth, born of the ruling classes,
sure of himself without conceit.   But in the other
faces in the group the eagerness that hurried his
classmates on and out of the village—some to
death, some to the West, some to sorrow—has no
counterpart on his gentle, earnest, manly face.

CHAPTER III

THE CALLOW YOUTH IN COLLEGE

After graduation at the Academy of Ludlow, and after a year's further preparation at another academy, he appeared at Amherst College, in Amherst, Mass., a freshman, utterly unmarked, even by his taciturnity, which was common enough, his quacking Vermont drawl, which was the common speech of scores of his fellows, nor by his Ludlow store clothes, with his trousers just a little bit too short and his coat just a trifle too long, and his ready-tied tie. His freckles were fading, and his hair, which had been red enough to give him the nickname of "Red," which he carried with the name of "Cal," did not distinguish him. Nor did the long nose and strong jaw of the Yankee youth mark his physiognomy among his fellows. He looked as Uncle Sam must have looked in his youth, before he grew his goatee and strapped his trousers under his boots—a typical Yankee with a face that seemed to throw back two centuries and restore the Puritan face of a vanishing race.

And with the Puritan face came the Puritan faith. Coolidge is a Congregationalist—a Yankee mystic. Enthroned but veiled, far back in his cosmic consciousness, in some Holy of Holies, there must reign despotically the symbol of Coolidge's deep belief in the moral government of the universe. Like the Emersonian credo, his belief came out of the Yankee soil, but it is none the less powerful because its roots are entwined in rocks. Now, this interpretation of life which men call faith thrust itself up from the depths of Coolidge's life inheritance while he was a student in Amherst.

Briefly let us consider Amherst. Thirty years ago it was a college of five hundred students with a faculty consecrated to the joy of service. This joy came from inoculating youth with the high passion for learning that dominates the lives of these men who have stepped apart from the world into the scholastic cloister. In Amherst two men wrestled with young Calvin Coolidge, according to the story of his contemporaries. The two men were Professor Morse in history and Professor Garman in philosophy. Morse made history the story of God's intention for the progress of the world. According to Morse, democracy was the climax of human institutions, because, forsooth, the voice of the people is the voice of God. And Garman taught the same thing in the terms of philosophy.

Consider this bashful, awkward, repressed youth coming down from the silent hills, out of a hard, but happy, life, wrestling in the hay meadow of a summer, wallowing through the snow in the sugar camps and with logging teams in the winter, reading

a few simple books well, wounded and awe-stricken
by the blows of death falling upon his life, dumb
and isolated in a gay and festive company of students, who in spite of their high purposes are, after
all, young and callow. Remember that he is an aristocrat by training and social position, a one-gallused
aristocrat, but real, even if he is not a pampered
child of fortune. Then remember always that the
frugality of a New England home is sending him
to college; that he lives in the cheapest boarding
house, in the barest room with no social graces
back of him, a wallflower at the few freshman functions which college custom compels him to attend.
And then, lo! there flooded into his life, there in the
college classroom, the light of a faith that life is
not a blank, that it "means intensely and means
good"; and this flood came at adolescence, when it
should come. It overflowed the springs of his conduct, watered all the shriveled purposes of a hard
New England heritage, and sent the sap of ambition
throbbing through his life. But it could not change
the granite exterior in which blood and environment
had enclosed his soul. His destiny was still marked
by Vermont. Said he, years later:

"Vermont is my birthright. My people there
are happy and contented. They belong to themselves, live within their income and fear no man."

When he was a man in middle life, after his life
had set upon its appointed path, he declared, "I have
never been able to find that any Coolidge ever went

COOLIDGE FATHER AND SON
"Many people don't understand why I am President," he paused and cackled
gently, "least of all my father."

(*Page 21*)

West." There you have it—a congenital lack of initiative—third word in the crossword puzzle—Caution! Coolidge speaks briefly, he believes deeply, and acts only when he has to. The bluster, the shifting opinions, the intrepid daring, that sometimes give glamour to American leadership, are congealed in Coolidge. So he is strong not as a leader of men but as an administrator.

All that life has developed under the wash of circumstance was on the plate there in Amherst. Slowly he injected himself into the college life. As a freshman he was an unnoticed unit of the student body—went along without distinction, without close comradeship, without apparent joy—a stranger in a friendly world. As a sophomore he delivered the Fourth of July oration at Plymouth—a callow youth with no particular message, and Colonel John Coolidge, *pater,* doesn't seem to have remembered it with much pride. "Many people," said Coolidge dryly to a friend recently, "don't understand why I'm President," he paused and cackled—"least of all my father!" A whole biography of family history lies dehydrated and preserved in those last few words! Yet the love between the two men—father and son —is one of the obvious things one sees when he knows either.

Going back to college for his second year, young Cal tried the girl proposition, but it would not work. The social lures of Smith College, so far as he was concerned, were futile. He gave up society. "None

of the Coolidges ever went West" or continued to
do things they did badly!

When he came back to school as a junior he began
to bloom. His trousers met shoetops, his coats conformed to the college mode. He appeared in the
consciousness of his fellow students as a person.
His silence was not broken. His lips still pursed as
though he had held them closed too long after a big
chew of tobacco. His wit—an acid effluvia out of
spiritual dried apples—was used for expression, not
for diversion. He appeared in the Plug Hat Race
of his class in a borrowed topper—and lost the race,
making a speech spiked with caustic wit that raised
the laughter of his classmen for him, and their
respect for him.

His record shows that he sedulously and in solemn
silence attended every class meeting. He became a
charter member of a new chapter of a college fra-
ternity, the Phi Gamma Delta, having been omitted
from the established fraternities, and, being a charter member, he shared leadership in the business
administration.

Turn back your memory and see his type, dear
reader, in your own college life; the solid, unsocial,
capable lad who did not quite make it and never
quite failed—the salt of the earth!

The college was giving him, not on the campus,
but in the classroom, a most unusual but highly practical form of education; Garman, the philosopher;
Morse, the historian, were making him their apostle,

were laying buttresses about his faith. No light person was this serious youth; no romantic figure even in his lonely walks; just a homespun man with some large vision lurching about in his soul and with a practical eye for the main chance, always squinting at a careless world. By way of irony, because they remembered his remarks in the Plug Hat Race in his junior year, his classmates at commencement elected him the Grove Orator, where he had to make the comic speech! He made it. It was aërated caustic acid!

The man who was voted by his class as the most likely to win fame was Dwight Morrow, later of the Morgan banking house. The keen discernment of Dwight Morrow is indicated by the fact that he voted the only vote in that contest for Calvin Coolidge, not dreaming that Coolidge would be President, but previsioning him as a Vermont legislator, congressman and probably life-term senator!

But Morrow did not pretend to know Coolidge even as a fellow classman. The two sprawling on the campus green in their pre-commencement days talked of plans; agreed that they were to be lawyers. But Coolidge declared he had no money to go to law school. Replying to Morrow's query as to where Coolidge would go, the youth answered laconically, "Northampton is the nearest courthouse!"

So there he went. He took the shortest line of least resistance: "None of the Coolidges ever went West." He read law in the office of Hammond &

Field—an old firm in Northampton, and there men saw the same lanky, grim, flint-visaged, blue-eyed youth that came down from Vermont to Amherst. He came into the law office characteristically. After he was introduced by an Amherst friend who spoke for Coolidge the Vermonter until he was out of breath, Coolidge let the elder lawyers talk themselves out of breath also. For at the end of the. interview they said he could come to the office and try his hand. He contributed just two words to the discussion, "Good morning!"

The next morning he appeared and went to reading Blackstone. A few weeks later Judge Field brought to the young law clerk a newspaper clipping from the Springfield *Republican* which announced that Calvin Coolidge of the law firm of Hammond & Field, of Northampton, had received the $150 gold medal awarded by the Sons of the Revolution for the best essay on "The Principles of the American Revolution."

"Is that you?" asked Field.

"Yes, sir," answered the clerk.

"When did you get it?"

"About six weeks ago," replied the lad.

"Why didn't you tell us?" insisted the judge.

"Didn't know you'd be interested," explained the apprentice. The judge looked his amazement and exclaimed:

"Have you told your father?"

"No. Sh'u'd I?" quacked the prize-winner and,

being admonished, notified his father. He said nothing more of the medal until a month later, when he asked the lawyers to put it into their safety deposit vault. Then a year or so later he laconically asked for it.

"We certainly have a queer duck in our office," said Judge Henry Field.

"An odd stick and hard to understand," said the other partner, Judge Hammond. "I had never seen just such a man—especially a young man. I couldn't understand how a man could be so quiet, and seem to care for nothing outside of his work!"

He was an odd stick even for New England, and that was in eastern Massachusetts, where they are supposed to make all the odd sorts and sizes.

As he emerged from childhood and youth into life he took life easy. The equation of his soul was set. He always took life easy. There at the spare table in the outer room of the best law office at Northampton, Calvin Coolidge, the young man, foreshadowed the man at his desk in the White House—calm, methodical, precise, deliberate, silent, a paragon of the cautious, respectable virtues. In him shone industry, thrift, economy, foresight and circumspection. But it was a bustling age; a time of adventure and enterprise in business, and in politics the Spanish War was setting us out on a long journey of imperial emprise. Big dreams were in the heart of America. It was not the Coolidge era. He had a quarter of a century to labor and to wait.

CHAPTER IV

OUR HERO STEPS OUT INTO LIFE

After two years of study in the law offices of Hammond & Field at Northampton, Mass., Calvin Coolidge was admitted to the bar and began his political career. He quietly got on the city Republican committee from the Second Ward, a strong Republican ward, and it may be assumed that he did not accidentally move into a strong Republican ward. He attended organization meetings, soberly, regularly, quietly, as he attended class meetings in Amherst, until the organization got used to seeing him. Then quietly, regularly, soberly he was elected to the city council from his ward. His first act was to introduce, soberly, regularly, quietly, a resolution of respect for the death of a Catholic colleague from a Democratic ward. Whereupon for many years after he was soberly, quietly and regularly strong at the election in that Democratic ward!

His law practice grew—also soberly, regularly, quietly. He made a specialty of the business of the small towns near Northampton; was reëlected to the council; got acquainted with the people of his ward; used to hang around the shoe shop and blacksmith shop where Democrats and Catholics who were strangers in Ward Two most often congregated; picked up their confidence, deserved it; did them all good turns when he could—and all quietly, regularly, soberly.

And then he ran for city solicitor, and because he had been frugal to the point of parsimony, without waste motion, without waste words and without waste friendship, he got all the Republican votes in Ward Two, all the "organization" votes from all over town, and the votes of a lot of Democrats whom he had met around at odd times doing odd jobs in his odd way. The surprise at his election broke out in a protest from a supporter of his opponent.

"Well, by Johnny, I never voted for you!"

"Ne'er mind," cackled Coolidge, quietly, regularly, soberly. "Somebody did!"

He had two terms as city solicitor and was appointed to the dignified office of court clerk, an office that carried money with it, distinction with it, promotion to the judiciary with it—the only appointive office, by the way, which Coolidge ever held. He tried it half a term and quit. The love of money was never in the Coolidge cosmos.

He always has respected money, defended wealth, deferred politically to the rights of property, but never has stopped his quiet, regular, sober pursuit of office to earn money, to accumulate wealth, or to possess any property. His frugality, which is of money—his own and other people's—of speech, of time, of endeavor, amounting often to bald parsimony, never has been turned to the accumulation of material things. His acquisitive faculty is marvelously developed. But it is for political service. Here is the key to his genius: The capacity for doing what he could do; the discernment which stopped him from biting off more than he could chew! Coolidge never tried a long jump.

Yet he held no low ideal of service. Now here we spell out the fourth word of the crossword puzzle; an eight-letter word meaning "All service is alike to God"—Idealism. A scrawny, stunted timber-line growth of idealism, but real, is Coolidge's. Behold the lanky man who quacks when he talks to save his diaphragm, a man with pursed lips who looks too preoccupied to expectorate; a spiritual hermit, greedy of his silence; a hedonist lolling in the lap of industry; a fanatic flagellating his emotions to numbness; a Yankee ascetic in small politics, following dumbly his meager aspirations as though ashamed of even their soft impeachment; climbing steadily, slowly through one little honorary office to another, seeking painfully, as a penitent walking over thorns, one starvation job after another that costs money which he earns by weary work; taking time which he hoards for himself like a miser, and faithfully, even generously, spending the fragrant years of his youth and the fruitful span of manhood in the dull day's work of almost petty political service. What a picture! There stands your ancient Puritan—cold-nosed, heavy-hearted, half-abashed, undramatic and wholly miserable, glorifying the main chance into a holy cause and so in the dull routine of a drab life laying the foundation of a noble civilization.

Coolidge, grinding through his long succession of minor village and state offices, was like that. Perhaps he was not consciously renouncing high honors, great power, desired affluence. Perhaps he just took, year by year, the job that he could do, the place that he knew he could fill; bashfully—or modestly maybe—fearing to reach for the larger plums. Poor he went in. Poor he came out, and un-rewarded by laurels. Yet something inside him held him to his task—some quenchless thirst for service that he could perform well, some thumping dynamo that would not slip its belt from the engine of his life. His master passion seemed to be to do the day's work so well that he might do to-morrow's work better. That was all there was to Calvin Coolidge. It was most commonplace, most unheroic, most humdrum, highly Yankee!—so like the soul of the barren hills of Vermont, prodigal in granite, rich in timber, giving bounteously but only for heart-breaking toil.

Calvin Coolidge, refusing the fat and ambitious office of court clerk, ran, the year of his refusal, for the state legislature. There he could serve. "The scriptural name for service," quoth old Garman in Amherst, "is love!" Then to get down to earth he says, "Property is coined service!" So Coolidge went out to service. And the bound-boy went to the husking in Boston with this note to the speaker of the Massachusetts house of representatives, from a mutual friend: "This will introduce Calvin Coolidge . . . a singed cat! . . . Anything you can do for him will be appreciated."

Coolidge evidently was a singed cat. He got no preference from the speaker. But one thing he knew he could do—so he did it. When he was thirty years old, in the full years of his discretion, when it was proper and seemly to do so, after his law practice had grown large enough to warrant it, Calvin Coolidge deliberately, quietly, soberly, married. He chose well—a teacher in the Clark Deaf and Dumb School, inured to silence— Miss Grace Goodhue, six or seven years his junior, a Vermonter, a graduate of the State University of Vermont, a splendid woman, vivacious, highly intuitive, charming and beautiful. She was his complement in every way. The two made a full team. A man who is wise in affairs of the heart need not fear folly in affairs of the head. Such wisdom brings luck. But it is dangerous. It excites the envy of fools, who are in the majority. If ever the fool vote had been amalgamated in America, Coolidge's luck would have changed.

To what extent Mrs. Coolidge has influenced her husband's judgments only two persons may testify. One is too silent to say, even if he realized it; and

the other too smart! But Mrs. Coolidge has accepted her husband's ideals and striven with him
to realize them. All her life she has been a poor
man's wife; has done her own work, sometimes even
her own washing, reared her own family and lived
the simple life with an honest man, surrounded, in
politics at least, by other women whose social greed
often has made their husbands grasping. But for
Mrs. Coolidge, her husband would not have traveled
the path he has climbed. If he had turned from it
at any point to make money, the charm of his luck
would have been broken. But because she was as
dear as he was wise, the Coolidges have been able
to live in one side of a semi-detached house which
they rented for $27 a month for fifteen years, and
for which they paid while he was in the White House
$36; with the principal of the high school occupy-
ing the other half. Also, while, and because the
Coolidges were living in this house on this modest
economical scale, they have risen in the political
scale from the state legislature to the White House.
To have paused one hour solely to make a dollar,
however honest, would have put an element of
selfishness into the Coolidge heart that would have
spoiled the record and corrupted him. The Coolidge
dollars were made incidentally, not as the first business of life.

We have come in this chronicle to a place where
a career begins in the life of Calvin Coolidge. It is
an astounding career, astounding in the insignifi-

cance of its outer details, astounding in the revela-
tion of its interpretation in terms of a man's aspirations.   Look at the man—spare, bashful, halting of
speech, with suppressed emotions, and with a frost-
bitten personality; such a man as Shakespeare described, who might have been cut out of a cheese
paring!   Let us look into the horoscope for a moment at this man's future: He goes to the state
legislature a couple of times from his home district, is elected mayor of his town by a lucky chance;
then being mayor naturally controls the nomination
when it is Northampton's "turn" to have a state
senator, a powerful office; allies himself with the
state boss, aspires to be president of the state senate, gets the job, is promoted to lieutenant governor,
holds the place for a few terms, is easily and almost inevitably promoted to the governorship, and
so, after reëlection, by a natural process becomes
Vice-President.   Then through death becomes President of the United States.

That career spells politics in its amiable moments,
with Lady Luck smiling upon a beloved child.   That
is the outer surface of the Calvin Coolidge career.
But if that outer surface were the motive and the
mainspring of the career it would have halted far
down the line.   It was the profoundly hidden things
in Calvin Coolidge's heart, the things that perhaps
no one but Grace Goodhue, his wife, and a few beloved friends ever have seen, that thrust Coolidge
to the presidency.   The key to the Coolidge

strength is a passion, a consuming inner fire, to serve—to serve the public and to serve in humble ways; so that he may be prepared to serve more largely.

For twenty-eight years, since he was committee-man of his party in Ward Two, in Northampton, he has been serving, and always unselfishly. There is the key to it—unselfishly. And that is strange, too—that a man who has been holding office for twenty-eight years should be unselfish. But here is the proof of his devotion; excepting one office which he left of his own accord, no office he has held in all these years carried a salary sufficient to keep him in decent comfort. And from no office has he got one single emolument, one good client, one stepping-stone to affluence. His private professional income remained that of a third-rate lawyer in a fourth-rate town. To come through a generation of office-holding to the White House, a poor man—yet never knowing the sting of poverty, missing nothing through wanting nothing, living in a rented duplex house next to a school teacher, to let his wife do her own cooking, nursing and washing, to scorn money, to forego social position, to loathe the arts of the demagogue and hold to a slow, harsh, grace-less speech, to come clean in a game where others are slimy with legal but ill-gotten gains; that record re-quires something more than common honesty. That record calls for some kind of hangdog consecration to service.

He is not merely a little man holding little jobs. Your little man is always grabbing at big jobs. Coolidge avoided big jobs, as jobs, until he was well prepared to do them! Here, unmistakably, is your Yankee mystic, the fanatic New England Brahmin, mad with his dogma but ashamed to speak of it. He has never revealed it. That is the Coolidge who has triumphed over his impediments of temperament, of inheritance, of environment. His belief in the sacramental character of public service has tyrannized over his life.

Perhaps the slow triumph of his creed has made him happy beneath his dour exterior, and so his happiness has made him wise—too wise to be good company for the frivolous.

CHAPTER V

THE FIRST RUNGS OF THE LADDER

When he came to the White House Calvin Coolidge, President of the United States, brought with him a lot of baggage from Plymouth and Ludlow, Vermont. He brought an abrupt Vermont way of opening conversation at exactly the point of greatest interest. In Ludlow—a mountain town of 3,000 or 4,000 with its textile mills where the French and the Italians form the industrial population, where 500 yards of store buildings house the commercial and professional life of the county, where in winter ox teams drag heavy sledges down from the hills, where the native population, in spite of the Celtic and Latin influences, remains as clearly English as it was before the Revolution—men attack things directly as Coolidge does. Around Ludlow men are rather inclined to regard the amenities of conversation—the embroideries by which we of other climes approach the matter in our hearts, the preliminaries of speech which concern the weather, the passing news of the day, and the obvious jockeying which we employ before turning into the matter near our hearts—as mere French palaver. The Plym-

outh neighbor who comes to borrow your hoe or
your horse says at the gate, "I have come to borrow
your hoe (or your horse)" and you tell him if he
can or he cannot have it and why. That being over,
if he is busy he goes, or if he isn't busy he stops and
discusses the weather or the things that float on the
surface of his heart.

When Coolidge first moved into the White
House, he was talking with an old stager in Republican politics about his difficulty in approaching
congressmen and senators and persuading them.
His first year of leadership was disastrous and he
knew it. Time and again Congress rose and defied
him, then defeated him.

"You must smile," said the congressional leader,
"when men come in. When they talk to you, look
them in the eye." Coolidge has a most intelligent
eye when he opens it, a most engaging countenance
when he exposes it, which inspires confidence.
"Don't sit looking out of the window when men
come to see you and lay their matters before you.
Turn toward them. Meet their countenances. You
needn't gab with them, but look interested."

But Ludlow inhibited him. Northampton had
taught him another kind of politics, and he was too
old to learn, too old to put the tricks of the West
and the South into his bag. He will go through to
the end as he began: the country statesman in Boston—just what he was when he went down from
Northampton to the state legislature.

In the Massachusetts legislature Calvin Coolidge made no brilliant record. The "singed cat" letter which he carried from his Northampton friend to the speaker of the house brought Coolidge no important committee assignments. The speaker made the common mistake that men make about Coolidge, of judging him by his exterior. So Coolidge served on two unimportant legislative committees, mercantile affairs and constitutional amendments. But he piously attended every committee meeting, as he had attended his class meetings in Amherst and his party organization meetings in Northampton—a dumb acolyte seeking the truth. They were dull, these committee meetings; but Coolidge scintillated rather feebly himself in those days. There he sat day after day, night after night, either in his committee room or in the legislative hall, taking the routine of the public business with terrible earnestness while others frivoled. Thus he husbanded his five talents. Being a faithful heart, he never missed the meetings of the joint committee of the house and senate—a sort of joint committee of the whole where public hearings occur on many important matters. This joint committee meeting of the two houses preserves the old town-meeting flavor in the Massachusetts legislature. Many legislators avoid these joint sessions. For most bills are made or doomed in smaller committees.

Coolidge learned much at these joint sessions, somewhat because he was an outsider in the smaller committees. He had no graces, no special abilities, no influence that first term. He was just a hard-plugging, average-minded man trying to get the hang of the legislative medium. He sensed, however, one important thing in that first session: that legislation, like kissing, goes by favors. Then conscientiously and by careful pains he applied this new wisdom to life. So when the speaker of the house, nursing a gubernatorial boom, came to Northampton, Coolidge met him, took the speaker around town, introduced him to the political leaders, and the next time Coolidge went up to Boston to make laws for the people, the speaker knew Coolidge. He got two real committees—banking and judiciary. He became an insider. He emerged. He duplicated his college career, in the legislature. He seems to have been interested in political matters rather than economic, in his second term. He worked on the law providing for the direct election of United States senators, for the direct primary, for woman suffrage.

His record that second year of his legislative term was that of a mild progressive. He supported bills providing for one day's rest in seven in industry, for reduced working hours for women and children, for lower railroad fares for workmen, for honest weighing in coal yards, for pensions for firemen's widows, and for municipal playgrounds. He spoke little, of course, but well, and took his job

with an earnestness that amounted to solemnity. He
lived at the Adams House, a cheap political hotel,
chummed with no one, belonged to no clique, avoided
the congregating places of what was known as "the
bunch," and went about his work with that simplicity and passionate sincerity of men who are
building better than they know. Of course he had
ambition, but he did not show it. If he ever had
a hankering for a good time, he did not look it. He
is described by his fellows of that day as punctual,
self-contained, deadly quiet, self-sufficient, caustic
under the prod, tireless but not enthusiastic, polite
but formal, ever ready to run an errand for a better
man in a good cause and not above expecting a returned favor for his cause, but never for himself.
He sought nothing for Coolidge; which was just as
well, for he lacked the charm which begets gratitude.

It is hard to say, in that first legislative session,
and it was hard to say nearly twenty years later in
the White House, whether Coolidge wanted nothing
or just did not know how to get it upon his graces
as a man. In that first session of the legislature
he saw fellow members using their places to advance
themselves in business. He saw his colleagues trading their own votes for good jobs for themselves.
The records show that he plodded on without reward. No one can tell if he had hope of reward.
Money and power did not tempt him. That is evident by every vote he cast. Yet he did not have the

radical's scorn for place and power. Always Coolidge has defended property politically, but has accumulated comparatively little of it for himself.

Looking at his legislative record those first years, one gets the impression of the close-fisted neophyte of some rigorous cult forever depositing his energy in some ethical bank, with a certain blind fatalism doing good turns for decent men and things like a miserly Vermont guardian of a trust, refusing to check out a penny for himself even in per diem. He came back to Northampton from his second legislative session poorer than he went, poorer in purse, but richer in experience and political standing. Possibly in his heart's heart he had some vague dream of future power. He may have gazed into the crystal ball of ambition, but what he saw he saw, and no one else knew it. He practiced law sedulously between legislative terms, but with no extraordinary success. Other lawyers complained that his fees were too modest. But if the signs of his self-esteem were low, he surely had the high self-respect of the modest man. He was a queer one, said the town of Northampton.

By the time Coolidge had been in Northampton a dozen years, he had been town councilman, city solicitor, clerk of the courts, chairman of the Republican City Committee, and member of the legislature. He had also been defeated for member of the school board. Four times in those years he had been before the people asking for votes. No haw-

hawing back-slapper was he at the hustings; but a rather poor hand-shaker. His method was to keep off Main Street as much as possible during a campaign and to see the people in their homes. He took the Republican wards for granted when he could, and sought to make inroads in the votes of the Democrats in their wards and bailiwicks. It was Coolidge's campaigning method to go into a house, speak briefly to the voter—or his wife if that was the best he could do—discuss no issues but state plainly that he was a candidate for the office, wanted the office and needed their votes. He wasted no words, made no promises, pretended no affection, but, having said his simple say, quietly backed out of the house, hat in hand, and went on to the next house. This he would do studiously, plodding by the hour up one street and down the next. It was a hard way to get votes. But it got them. And so as the years passed, Northampton came to know its bashful son.

CHAPTER VI

ECCE THE SMALL-TOWN HOMO

And here we must sketch Northampton. For as the years go, Vermont fades out of his background into his inheritance, and Northampton begins to assimilate Coolidge. Northampton twenty years ago was a town of 20,000 people, or such a number. A three-phase town—a college town, a farming town, an industrial town. The college and the farms contributed the native stock to the town; the industries brought the Irish, who are not always strong enough to govern a town. But they added a charm to its politics and a tithe to its taxes and played the game like good sportsmen. Moreover, they furnished a final proof that Coolidge was and is more than a long-nosed Yankee Brahmin: he got on with the Irish. Often they voted for him; always they respected him. He and they, being essentially politically minded, understood one another.

This understanding broadened as his career opened. Years later he was friendly with the ruling cardinal in Boston. Deeply in Calvin Coolidge's heart lies some affinity for the gay loyalty of an

Irishman. Perhaps Coolidge loves the daring which
he lacks. But in spite of the foreign-born minority
which somewhat dominated Northampton two decades ago, one must not forget that Northampton
was and is a country town; a town of elm-bordered
streets and lawns, of wooden houses, some colonial
and beautiful, others modern and most comfortable;
houses wherein lived in those days a self-respecting,
free-born race. Northampton, like every other
American country town, has its silk-stocking Republican ward, and another ward or two a few cuts under
this silk-stocking ward socially and industrially that
generally go Democratic. Coolidge lived from the
beginning of his Northampton career in the silk-
stocking ward, Ward Two, the Republican ward.
Here Smith College thrives with its 2,000 students
appertaining. In Ward Two live a middle-class
white, Nordic, sophisticated and self-sufficient race
on an average income per family of something under
$3,000 a year. Massasoit Street, Coolidge's home
for nearly twenty years, is a typical residential street
in a typical Republican ward in a typical American
country town. Here live the merchant, the doctor,
the lawyer, the teacher, the professor, the head
clerk, the superintendent, the banker, and the retired farmer.

Well might the story of the life and career of
Calvin Coolidge have a sub-title, "The Adventures
of a Man from Massasoit Street." For Coolidge
is and always will be Massasoit Street incarnate—

the high-caste country town man with the aristocrat's penchant for democracy: a man who loves his
fellow men because he lives with them and understands them. If one could forget Coolidge's Yankee
twang, his habit of repression, his greed for silence—which are, after all, the merest externalities
of his character—one could understand him best by
regarding him as a country-town man. Northampton differs only in a few externals from the
country town of Michigan, of the Carolinas, of the
Dakotas, or of the Coast. But it differs deeply and
fundamentally from the country village and the first-
class city. So, in considering Coolidge, however
taciturn he may seem, we must remember him as the
man who walks to work every morning, nodding to
his fellow townsmen whom he knows; stopping in
the business part of the town upon an errand, pick-
ing up apparently useless information, and putting
it in his heart to return one day a treasure—the
knowledge of the times, the knowledge of the folks.

One finds Coolidge in his speeches and writings
trying to avoid the word "people": he uses the
phrase "the folks," somewhat because "the people"
is the demagogue's whip-cracker and because "the
folks" is more familiar and a bit affectionate. Certainly he would not transport his beloved folks to
the liberal heaven, where business is benevolently
guarded by justice. He would give them good business and let the devil take the bankrupts. Yet no
man can understand the folks so well as Coolidge

understands the people of his country town, which epitomize all country towns and most of America— and not love the folks. Being what he is, a steam engine could not drag from him an expression of affection. But the folks he loves and understands are the folks he loved and understood in Plymouth, Ludlow and Northampton. Politically he thinks in terms of these environments. He sees that a few cents difference in the tariff on suit linings throws tens of thousands of workers out of employment who work in the mills back home. So the tariff is a sacred institution to him. He says little about it, but he is adamant before a suggestion of lower tariff on anything. It does not occur to him that perhaps a reorganization of the finances of the mill-owners might justly be demanded, that tariffs should not be imposed upon consumers all over the land to pay fixed charges and dividends upon overcapitalization in the guise of keeping men at work in the mills. He only sees idle, hungry people and sees that the tariff will feed them.

These are facts; the rest, theories. Moreover, the theories upset vested rights. Plymouth, Ludlow and Northampton waste no time in considering justice when they should be promoting business. The evils of the open saloon in the country town strike Coolidge as economic waste, so he is a strong prohibitionist. He will enforce the law at all costs of men and treasure. To his knowledge have come scores of instances wherein the immigration laws do cruel injustice to individuals, separating families because national quotas are filled, and the cruelty of it touches his tender heart, for Coolidge is essentially a tender-hearted man. So that problem, a concrete problem, a country-town problem, touches him. All this must be set down when we consider Coolidge of Northampton on his way to Washington, D. C.

There are few revealing things in the life of this country townsman, either written or spoken or exposed in deeds. He has a molelike modesty, partly a bashful complex, partly a habit of life. But sometimes he does uncover himself in his writings and speeches, and once in Amherst, talking as governor of Massachusetts about politics, he said a blunt, frank, almost brutal thing about the participation of college men in politics. He was asked if there were any special obligation of a college man to be a candidate and answered, "I do not think so," then he continued with dry, caustic Yankee sarcasm:

"It is said that although college graduates constitute but 1 per cent of our population, they hold 50 per cent of the offices, so this question seems to take care of itself. But I do not feel that there is any more obligation for a college man to run for office than there is to become a banker, merchant, or a teacher. Some men have a particular aptitude and some have not for politics. Experience counts here as in any other human activity. . . . If an individual finds he has liking and capacity for his work in politics, he will involuntarily find himself engaged in it. There is no catalogue of such capacity. One man gets results in his life

COOLIDGE AS MAYOR OF NORTHAMPTON

"He could not have been wise enough to know, in his thirties, that promotion from one trivial office to another would make him President in his forties."

(Page 47)

in one way, another in another. But, in general, only the man of broad and deep understanding of his fellow men can meet with much success in politics."

This, coming ten years ago from a man supposed to be hard, crabbed, aloof and self-centered, is a denial, a deep convincing denial, of that phase of the Coolidge myth. He is silent. He is probably struggling forever with some kind of devil that holds him back from the warmer contacts of life. But he is not the mythical Coolidge of his enemies any more than he is the mythical Coolidge of the seven million majority. Politics as he has revealed it in this quotation, has become the inevitable urge of his life. To him politics is what the sea is to the sailor, the woods to the forester, the family to the mother, an instinctive passion for some kind of service. All of which sounds highty-tighty, as though Coolidge had Sir Galahad's complaint, and was going to become a bronze statue overnight and stand in the park to encourage good young men. He merely has some kind of inner demon, not openly ambition—for he does not walk the ways of a patently ambitious man—which keep him doing humble political tasks so well that promotion always follows each service, because he is obviously prepared for promotion. He has accepted promotion modestly, and probably without much conscious seeking of promotion, certainly with no crafty prescience of where promotion would carry him. He could not have been wise enough to know, in his thirties, that this gradual promotion from one trivial office to another would make him President in his late forties. An ambitious man would have headed for Congress or the United States Senate, or the judiciary, in his thirties. But Coolidge kept jogging along, mincing his way politically, with short, dainty steps, but always forward.

After Coolidge had served two terms in the state legislature, opportunity came for him to run for mayor of Northampton. Northampton was his legislative district. He was coming to know the people fairly well, and they him—a reserved, industrious, rather kindly, spare, simple young man, modest in his straight walking gait, without knee action or strut in it, who hurried directly from one errand to another along the business streets, who appeared rarely in the courts, and who attended regularly the Jonathan Edwards Congregational Church of which his wife was a member and in which he was a rather inconspicuous but ever-present brother-in-law.

Among his other clients—who were not numerous, for he did not conspicuously succeed as a lawyer—was the Springfield Brewery. He gave it no political service; it was his business to look after its barkeepers in the courts. Sometimes he appeared for its drunks in the police court and advised and defended its representatives in other local controversies with the powers that were in Northampton. And here appears smiling Lady Luck for the first time in Coolidge's life. A men's club was organized in the Jonathan Edwards Congregational Church in which were debates on topics of current interest. The pastor, in 1909, desired a debate upon the question of license or no license for the saloons. Mr. Harry E. Bicknell, a promising young Northampton statesman, being a member of the church, told the pastor that it would be impossible to get any one to take the anti-saloon side of the question —what we now call the dry side. On the day that Bicknell first talked to the pastor about the debate, Bicknell promised, by way of being a good Congregationalist and a good sport, to take either side of the debate. After a week's hard trial, the pastor could find no one else to talk against saloons and turned to Bicknell to help the club. He took the dry side. Being a man of earnestness and ardor, he debated with a certain eloquence and emphasis. To him it was a purely academic debate, but it aroused the enmity of the wet element in the town. Within a few months, having forgotten all about the debate, Bicknell declared himself as a candidate for mayor. But the wets hadn't forgotten his eloquence and emphasis. The more Bicknell tried to explain the circumstances of the debate, the more he lost the few dry votes in town and the more the wets concluded that he would not do to tie up to—a rather preposterous conclusion under the circumstances, but one which most voters make in trying to simplify issues in terms of men.

Then came the urge from the wets for the young attorney of the Springfield Brewery to enter the race for mayor. Coolidge entered the race. One of his favorite quotations is from Franklin's declaration that public office should neither be sought nor refused, but he did not make the wet issue. He avoided that issue—which was the chief issue in the campaign. He talked about principles of government, about city administration in the abstract, when he talked at all, which was precious little. He relied upon the Republican silk-stocking respectable vote in Ward Two to back him because he was of it, and his reliance was wise. Then he relied upon his friends, the Irish, who had more or less been with him in the other wards, to stay with him, and his reliance there was wise. And he knew that his friends, the barkeepers employed by the brewery company and the drunks and the down-and-outs whom he had defended and advised, would probably be with him; but he took no chances. He was thorough. So he took up his house-to-house canvass in the Democratic industrial wards. In that heated campaign when he was getting wet votes by the hundreds, he did not change his technique of vote-seeking. In simple, direct language which the men whom he had befriended could not mistake, he asked them for their votes. He made no plea about principles of administration, indulged in no tall talk about reform, did not refer to his adversary in any re-

mote way, but spoke in his dry, harsh, nasal voice,
saying:

"I want your vote. I need it. I shall appreciate
it."

Then, if debate or controversy arose upon the
disagreeable issue of the campaign, he answered
questions in monosyllables, being careful to inject
the issue no further into the discussion. He kept
the heart of his friend upon the Coolidge need for
a vote. It was rather an undramatic pilgrimage for
a knight-errant of democracy, but Coolidge won by
a rather larger majority than usually is given to
mayoralty candidates.

The mayor's office carried no adequate compensation, and required a lot of hard work which he
did well. Indeed, he made a good mayor by doing
nothing in particular with great economy. The
Springfield Brewery had no more favors from him
than the Women's Christian Temperance Union. It
could not be said, at the end of his first term, that
Coolidge had paid any political debts in the mayor's
office, except his common debt to the common people
who elected him.

Life to Coolidge has been a perpetual process
of education. He went to school in the mayor's
office at Northampton and learned something about
taxation. It is odd that a man who never has had
money should be interested in money. Until he was
past fifty Coolidge never paid a dollar's worth of

real-estate taxation and precious little income taxes. Yet on the subject of taxation he will break his habitual silence and babble like a boy. In the mayor's office it was said of him that he was greedy to save time, greedy to save words, and greedy to save taxes. Yet one must not get the idea that he was a pale recluse, living the life of a Sunday-school hero, with exemplary regularity. Once every blue moon he sat down in one of the gardens of Northampton, took a single, solemn glass of beer— this, of course, before the days of the great Volstead drouth—cracked a single, solemn joke, drier than the pretzel that he munched, and felt that he had for that day and season done his full social duty to God and man.

If a politician failed him, Coolidge avoided that politician in his next alliance. So tradition in North-ampton concluded that the remote strain of Indian blood in him left a thin strain of vindictiveness, which is probably not true. It is merely the burned child avoiding the fire. But because he never ex-plained, never elaborated his reasons, not even after he acted, as liars do, Coolidge acquired a reputation which lingers around Northampton of being a bit mean in spots. This reputation was the popular interpretation put upon the reaction of the cautious man to his unreliable fellows.

He worked hard at the mayor's job, meeting the multitude rather distantly, but never haughtily. He was only shy—not proud. No one ever slapped him on the back.   Yet no one ever presented a problem that he did not try to solve; no one asked a favor that he could grant which was refused.   He was always on call, always serving.   Apparently he had no vacation, no diversion, no felicitous moments of gay introspection.   Yet with this queer exterior—a sort of impediment in his social manners, not a flaw in his character—he was a vote-getter; somewhat as a cripple is by reason of his affliction.   So serving his time as mayor for two years at hard labor, without financial reward, yet all the time bearing in mind the finances of his masters, conserving property yet obeying some inner monastic vow against owning much property, Calvin Coolidge prepared for the next upward step in his career.

Here we find him retiring as mayor of the town where he has lived for fifteen years, little changed by time and circumstance.   He is well into his fortieth year.   He has saved a little money—a precious little as money goes in his class and cult in America; a few thousands, perhaps a few ten thousands.   Spiritually he is static.   He is what he was in Ludlow, even in Plymouth.   Politically he is like a wave.   He seems to be moving, but it is not far forward.   He is in reality gathering political energy, charging his political batteries.   He is a rather lonely but not a friendless figure in Northampton as its mayor.   He has no enemies, has taken part in no factional fighting, espoused no causes, broken no regular alignments.   He is a modestly successful country-town politician; always obliging but never obstreperous, decently ready but never excited about running for public office, though never holding an office of any profit or much power. Never was he insignificant, but always he seems to have been negligible in those days of his thirties in Northampton. What plans he had for his public life, no one knew, no one suspected. He uttered no noble phrases. If he had his high visions they did not glow through the mask of his countenance. So far as his friends knew, he doused his visions with his silence. His soul cast no portentous shadow. He was, there at the height of his manhood, nine years only before entering a national career, what he was in the beginning and ever shall be, a plain, an unvarnished New England gentleman with no nonsense about him—fit for any duty, but seeking no power of place.

PART II

FOR THEY SHALL INHERIT
THE EARTH

CHAPTER VII

THE FIRST APPEARANCE OF THE COOLIDGE MYTH

"What is your hobby?" asked a Washington lady of Calvin Coolidge who had at the time just stepped into his tenth consecutive political position in a quarter of a century.

"Holding office," cackled the dry Presidential voice in the answer which was considered a good joke in those latitudes.

But it was no joke. Coolidge never jokes. He is brief, and brevity is the soul of wit, but with Coolidge wit is a mere by-product of brevity. And this is a queer, deeply significant thing about him: He thrives on his by-products. He made his living out of law. He had made his life out of politics. He learned little and earned little at the bar. The law, to which he has devoted himself earnestly, has yielded him barely board and clothes and a roof for his family. Politics, which he followed as a diversion, as a hobby if you will, taught him how to be useful and gave him fame. Always we must bear in mind in considering the Coolidge career that politics was financially a liability to Coolidge. He held only offices of honorary service; at the best, of

meager salaries. But he dallied with these offices
so steadily, so sedulously that his income from the
law was smaller than his talent may have justified.
He never had a chance to develop his earning capacity because of the time he wasted on his usefulness.
Councilman, city solicitor, court clerk, legislator,
mayor he was, all in a decade, and came through it
with no dollar sticking to his fingers or a client
haunting his office out of politics. Yet he was no
fool, even according to thrifty New England stand-
ards. He accumulated something as he went along
—if little money, then much fame.

In his two terms as mayor, Calvin Coolidge did
one rather definite thing. He solidified himself
with the Republican organization of his town. He
was a Republican mayor—not a biased, contentious
Republican, but deeply dependable. He alienated
no Democratic support. He held his Democratic
friends, but after nearly two years in the mayor's
office he was the unanimous choice of the Republican
leaders of his senatorial district for the Republican
state senatorial nomination. He accumulated political capital. The direct primary had come to
Massachusetts somewhat through Coolidge's aid
in the legislature, certainly with his support and
approval. Northampton was in a district containing other towns, and a rotation had been established
under the old convention system among the towns—
passing the senatorial office around. It was Northampton's turn in 1912 to have a state senator. The

unanimous support of the district leaders gave Coolidge the primary nomination without opposition. His two terms as mayor had distinguished him sufficiently to make that support easy. His election was no difficult matter in 1912, though that was the year of the Roosevelt separation from the Republican Party. Coolidge had supported the Roosevelt wing of the party more or less, but he did not leave the party with the Roosevelt bolt.

He went into the state senate with some distinction and with a valuable acquaintance among his senatorial colleagues, many of whom he had worked with in the assembly. He came back to Boston as state senator—again settled himself in the Adams House, where he had stopped as a member of the assembly, and was the same quiet, enigmatic, remote and kindly Puritan who had worked in the lower house.

His methods had not changed in three years, if his acquaintance had widened. Others may have misunderstood him; but let it not be assumed that he did not understand his fellows. He had measured them all, knew what was each man's heart's desire in politics, and where Coolidge could, he rather gently but never awkwardly, offered help. This had been his way in the legislature; he developed it in the senate. He asked for nothing, gave much, but kept one thing inviolate: his word. Politicians will quickly recognize this type. He made few promises and broke none. His taciturn habit

made it easy for him to check up on his outstanding
obligations.   He kept true to his type.   He knew
exactly what his political liabilities were and perhaps knew how slight were his assets in public
esteem, for he had no blarneying ways with him, no
charm, no social graces.

A "singed cat" he was when he went to Boston
to the legislature, a "singed cat" he was when he
left Boston for the White House.   Yet it must not
be assumed that Coolidge, with all his remoteness
from men, was not near to the heart of things.   He
knew on which side his bread was buttered politically.   Senator Coolidge sponsored a bill which provided for interurban trolleys in the small towns of
his section and put it through.   It was essentially
a farmer's bill; for it widened the dairy farmer's
market.   So the farmers came to know Coolidge
well and favorably, not Coolidge the man, but the
Coolidge trade-mark, the thing which stands for
service in politics.

Then along came the great strike of 1913 at
Lawrence among the textile workers.   Coolidge was
chairman of a senate committee appointed to consider the strike.   It was almost an arbitration committee.   It did function in settling the difference between the management and the trade union.   The
work of the committee made Coolidge known in Boston.   It is interesting to watch this career of the in-
defatigable Vermonter getting on in Massachusetts.
He was molelike in his silence, yet because of his

dumbness perhaps what seems like instinct was a heavily reasoned, logical determination to move to a certain goal. That his goal was the Presidency is an absurd conclusion. No one knows what the goal was, least of all Calvin Coolidge. Coolidge's life, like all lives, a changeless exact quality of personality—let us call it X in the equation—moved with a definite direction, plus circumstance, plus environment, plus the influence outside ourselves that we call Fate by which we are fitted into our niche in the machinery of Progress. Coolidge there in the senate, in his first state senatorial term, served the farmers and made a reputation in Boston. At the same time, honestly, conscientiously he did each day's work according to the dictates of the New England conscience. Through this incident we may discern the spiritual skeleton of the man at that time —an instinct for following cautiously, but with scrupulous honesty, the path of the main chance illuminated by an enlightened self-interest.

Considering Coolidge as the crossword puzzle we have come this far: from his blood and environment in Vermont he had silence, industry, economy, honesty and a mysticism that we call faith in the moral government of the universe. These things they knew about Coolidge in Northampton before he had been there a dozen years. They learned these things in Boston during his two terms in the assembly and one term in the senate. And then to the crossword puzzle they added a passionate repressed sincerity. For this sincerity he was known of men also, but his passion was deeply inward, never outwardly visible. Its outward expression was negative. Never was he a bluffer, not even a poseur! He could not pose any more than he could babble! Either would reveal him; hence he avoided both pose and chatter. He never claimed as much as he did, and so got credit for doing more than any human could do. Humanity is that way. Thus the superman myth arose! "Blessed be the meek, for they shall inherit the earth" is one of those deeply fundamental truths about mankind—humorous, pathetic, terrible; but divinely spoken. The Coolidge type, lacking strong outlines, or clearly appraised proportions, easily takes on, through the self-made hypnosis of man, heroic, gigantic proportions. That is how the meek came into the inheritance, while the angels rock with laughter at man's stupidity.

Under the code in the Northampton senatorial district a state senator was entitled to a second term. Coolidge had that with small opposition. He went back to Boston and the Adams House, chairman of the railroad committee, a vital part of the organization of the senate.

He had emerged in Boston. But Boston never cared for Coolidge. His twelve years' residence in Boston found him still an outsider. Back Bay Boston never forgave him the Adams House, which was equivalent to saying that it could not tolerate simple honesty, complicated with a desire for the main chance. If Coolidge could have allowed himself to acquire a wealthy client whose fees would have sent Coolidge to a first-class hotel or given him a Boston or even a Northampton house, Back Bay might have accepted him because of his Puritan physiognomy, his three hundred years of American ancestry and his New England twang. If Coolidge knew that he was not accepted in the inner shrine of the Sacred Codfish, he did not let it influence him. He held no grudges, made no enemies and ignored Back Bay as completely as Back Bay rejected him. He ignored it profoundly—even to the extent of serving it when he thought it should have service. Every Saturday he rode in the day coach up to Northampton to spend Sunday, and every Monday he came back in the day coach, sitting if he could in a seat alone, smoking a stogy cigar or two, avoiding conversation if he could, perhaps thinking, perhaps indulging in deep and silent vegetation. Fellow senators and members of the legislature rode with him on the train. If a man had a favor to ask, he asked it of Coolidge, got a grunt or a quack in reply which meant nothing, and if it were a decent favor in a few days the man found that it had been granted, and marveled at what manner of man this silent creature was who performed without flourish, made good without seeming to desire credit or even acknowledgment, and who, in return, because of his curious wordless ways bound his fellows to him with hoops of steel.

In considering Calvin Coolidge in the days of his political youth we must always remember the political soil from which he sprang. Outwardly he had ceased to be a Vermonter in 1914. He was of Massachusetts. Massachusetts was an honest, forward-moving state politically. The state government had few scandals in those years. The Republican machine was decent as machines go, decent in that it did not encourage crookedness, graft, or extravagance. It was a vindictive machine in that it punished its enemies. It was a wicked machine in that it rewarded its unworthy friends, often immoderately, sometimes immorally, at the public expense.

But the Massachusetts machine did not require that a regular conforming Republican in office shall do nefarious things, as party machines in other states often have held their public servants to unspeakable performances. Coolidge, who was a mild liberal, or perhaps better, a liberal conservative in his first years of political life, ran with the machine without exactly joining it, without consciously acknowledging it.

In those days, Senator Murray Crane, the paper manufacturer, was the head of the Massachusetts Republican machine; a capitalist who spoke the language of his class and who conducted in Massachusetts an honest plutocracy—at least as honest as the times would permit. Spiritually, there was much in common between him and Coolidge. Crane had in him a certain elementary taciturnity which never

COOLIDGE AS LIEUTENANT-GOVERNOR

"He was like any two-legged, soft-spoken wood-hewer or water-drawer in local politics."

(*Page 65*)

quite developed, for often he chattered. But he understood the Coolidge silence, appraised his man, found that his word was not merely at par but far above par in the state senate. Crane marked Coolidge for promotion, and the fact that Coolidge was interested, quietly but effectively, in those things which Roosevelt clamored for—the primary, the regulation of child labor and of the hours of service for women, the recognition of labor unions, the direct election of United States senators, mothers' pensions and those legal ameliorations of the condition of the under-privileged known as "social and industrial justice," did not lessen the value of Coolidge in Crane's eyes. As the leader of a machine, what he wanted was a dependable man, a discreet man, an industrious man. If the man happened to have what Crane regarded as a slight crazy streak, no matter. In the chief essentials Coolidge fitted, and so became a cog in the machine.

Now they will tell you in Northampton, those who control its Republican politics, that the leaders did not consider Coolidge seriously during the first dozen or fifteen years of his political career. He was like any two-legged, soft-spoken, persistent wood-hewer or water-drawer in local politics; doing fairly well, serving efficiently but not astonishingly the purposes for which he was elected, the people who employed him. As a lawyer he developed no great talent and acquired no large practice. He was not a familiar figure on the Northampton streets, except at election time when he avoided the main streets and kept up his habit of making a house-to-house campaign, somewhat a back-door campaign. As councilman, legislator, mayor and state senator, slowly rising never pausing in his political ascendency, he attracted no special notice of the men who were responsible for Republican majorities in Northampton. He always was with them. He was a lone figure who made no pretense of playing a lone hand. He served the party when he could and did more than he promised. Also he told the members of his party's organization only as much of his policies and plans as he thought was good for them, which was miserably little. So he closed his second term in the state senate, which, according to the code, was all that was coming to him.

Then, for the first time in Coolidge's career, a "Coolidge went West." He did an unusual thing. He sought a third term in the state senate. He seemed canny about it. The speaker of the senate was running for reëlection. He had opposed woman suffrage with acerbity. It looked to Coolidge and to others who were watching the cards on the polit-ical table as though the speaker of the senate would be defeated at the polls. The defeat would leave his office vacant. Coolidge insisted upon a third nomination. The vote of Northampton controlled the primary. He was easily nominated. The old "gentleman's agreement" for the rotation of the senatorial nomination was broken. But there was little political rancor. Coolidge's election in November was not in doubt, though a third term was unusual. Apparently Coolidge had his eye on the returns from the speaker's district more avidly than upon his own district. During election night the returns came in, indicating Coolidge's election and also the speaker's defeat. Coolidge took the eight o'clock train the next morning, said nothing to any one, possibly not even to Mrs. Coolidge—though that is unthinkable—went down to Boston, laid his case before Murray Crane, the Republican state boss, had Crane's promise of support for the speakership of the state senate, and the two on the long-distance telephone tied up the speakership within two days.

Then Coolidge came home the second night the acknowledged victor in the race. The speaker of a Republican senate was one of the titulary leaders of the Republican Party in the state, outranked only by the governor. Coolidge emerged in Massachusetts a state leader, a man of parts and consequence. Then for the first time Northampton and those who had smiled tolerantly at the slim, lean-faced, rasping-voiced, monosyllabic creature who had been their state senator, their mayor, their legislator, their city councillor and their councilman, attracting somewhat smaller notice than a wooden Indian on the street, began to marvel at what manner of man he was. They began to wonder how he had done it; what were his methods. So they invoked the fickle goddess Lady Luck to explain the rise. Thus the first Coolidge myth—the legend of the lucky man—began to form!

Simultaneously with the first Coolidge myth appeared the second Coolidge myth of the superman —the stern, hard, all-wise, omnipotent, omniscient, immutable creature who only needs whiskers and a throne to be the incarnation of the Puritan deity. Between these two myths—one of the fool for luck and the other of the angel of light—lies the truth about the man Coolidge.

But "Pilate saith unto him, what is truth?"

CHAPTER VIII

Calvin Coolidge became President of the United States largely because he had a college degree. That degree represented a certain training of his mind, a certain habit of attention toward the printed page, a certain familiarity with the wisdom of humanity stored in books. But he might have obtained this training, this capacity for attention and even the wisdom of the ages without a college degree. The college degree helped him because it made him an alumnus of Amherst, and in 1914 the Amherst alumni took hold of Coolidge's destiny.

That year Judge Henry Field, of Northampton, and Frank W. Stearns with half a dozen of the alumni were sitting around a table in Boston, grumbling because "the Harvard crowd" in Massachusetts, by standing together and boosting Harvard men, was getting too far in state politics and business affairs. From the grumbling rose this resolve: pick up some Amherst man and try boosting him. It is probable that Judge Field, of Northampton, under whom Coolidge had studied law, in response to the question "name your man," suggested Calvin Coolidge, "a bright young man in his late thirties, former member of the legislature, former mayor, and at the time chairman of the railroad committee of the senate and a power of the first magnitude in the organization of the legislature." Frank Stearns, somewhere in the identification of Coolidge which Judge Field was giving, asked "Who's Coolidge?" and being told, replied: "Well, all right. If you say Coolidge, it's Coolidge, but the only time I ever met him he insulted me."

(Parenthetically, let us consider the insult. In 1913 Stearns walked into Coolidge's committee room in the office of the Boston senate with a bill calling for some consideration for Amherst College. Stearns was one of the leading dry goods merchants in Boston and a guardian angel of Amherst. An apochryphal version of the story declares that when Stearns came in Coolidge unlocked a closet and brought out a chair for Stearns. But this probably is the romantic verisimilitude added to the fable by some artistic nature. At least Senator Coolidge listened to Mr. Stearns's plan. Being an Amherst man, it was presumed that Coolidge would grant the request. When Stearns had completely run down and had nothing more to say, Coolidge spoke, briefly, as follows:

"Too late. Time for consideration of new business has passed."

Just that! To get the effect of it on Stearns, quack it sharply.

A pause followed during which Stearns found his hat and got out of the room. Then, declares the artistic chronicler, Coolidge locked up the chair again. That was the insult. But at the next session of the legislature, without having said a word to Stearns about it, Coolidge made that bill his first business and it was passed early in the session.)

The upshot of the conference of the Amherst men was that the Amherst crowd in Boston gave a dinner to Coolidge and Stearns fell in love with him. Now State Senator Calvin Coolidge, of Northampton, strangely enough, was a lovable creature—for all his mute ways. He conformed to two types in politics—the man obsessed by his promises, who often is of the silent type, and also the man who loves to do errands—your political messenger boy. But alas, generally the political messenger is a braggart, too, highly appreciating his own services. Coolidge kept his word, ran errands for others and was actually modest. There is nothing of the Uriah Heep in Coolidge; his modesty does not cringe. It is gentle but firm, and stands no contumely. He will not be "put upon," and only from fools is he likely to get insult; for always about his modesty there is a foundation of rather hard and wholesome self-respect. He did errands in the state senate; errands for Murray Crane, but also errands for the humblest senator from a Boston district, errands for members of the assembly, errands for the prevalent governor, who during Coolidge's early state senatorial career happened to be a Democrat. Coolidge was willing to help any man in any decent endeavor. He was laying up political capital—the miser! And the fact that Coolidge never bragged about his achievements, never gave the impression that he was a "power" in the state senate, never complained, idly as boasters complain, about the ingratitude of his fellows, in effect, gave to his political capital all the quality of hoardings—secret treasure! No one knew how rich he was in political strength; few suspected. But Frank Stearns knew. He watched Coolidge; kept books on Coolidge's errands; became his political banker.

It is part of the puzzle which men call the Coolidge luck, that as president of the Massachusetts state senate he was for a year or more the ranking Republican in his state. The governor and the lieutenant governor were Democrats. The Roosevelt bolt of 1912 to 1914 had split the Republican vote, and so Coolidge, luckily, being president of the senate, was responsible for the party record. That is why he wrote the Republican platform which we shall consider later. His position of leadership in Massachusetts gave him much political power. And he used it, not for Calvin Coolidge, the lawyer of Northampton, not for the father of the Coolidge children that they might have a better home, not for any immediate material gain for Calvin Coolidge the man; but for Calvin Coolidge the politician he was greedy enough—though as it were surrep-

titiously. Frank Stearns saw the deposits mounting
up day by day in Coolidge's political bank and
Stearns knew therefore that Coolidge had a future.
Stearns's faith in Coolidge was not so blind as it
sometimes seemed. His faith was the faith of a
canny and knowledgous man.

Let us consider Stearns; height five feet six inches,
weight 190 pounds, perhaps 10 pounds more or 10
pounds less, age possibly 65; himself rather a silent
man, though not fanatic about it, who had been in
charge of the publicity of an important dry goods
house for several years; who knew all the tricks and
manners of public appeal and who, being delighted
with the final performance of Coolidge in the Amherst matter, sought him out. Stearns and Coolidge
have found the affinity of opposites. Stearns, heavy-
set, heavy-eyed, heavy-voiced, heavy-footed, delighted in the spare, keen-eyed, sharp-voiced, quick-
moving Coolidge. The two must have sat many silent hours smoking, like two horses, cross-necked in
the corner of a pasture, getting acquainted without
words! Finally the spiritual bridge was completed
between them and they lived happily ever after.
Across that bridge flows the commerce of a beautiful affection. No man gets far in this world whose
capacity for affection is dwarfed. Our Presidents
have all been affectionate men. Harding spilled his
heart upon scoundrels; Wilson loved men, not wisely
but too well, and being bored with them cast them
off ruthlessly. Roosevelt took men into his heart

by the score and so long as they were true, held them in spite of their faults. McKinley's major passion was Mark Hanna, and McKinley was the apple of Hanna's eye. Stearns was the Fidus Achates in the affair with Coolidge. If Stearns asked nothing, Coolidge gave him in return for his unselfishness a single-hearted and constant affection.

In 1915, in Coolidge's third term as state senator, Stearns began his promotion of the Coolidge career with advertising methods through the impulse of the Amherst group. Stearns tried hard to persuade Coolidge to run for lieutenant governor. It was the next obvious step ahead of the Northampton state senator. Coolidge refused to be persuaded. Stearns was persistent, but got in return only some sort of a nasal staccato declaration that to-day's work was more important than to-morrow's hope, only not epigrammatically. Coolidge rarely speaks epigrammatically; he speaks with a brevity that sometimes boils down to epigrams as an incident of brevity. All Stearns could do in those days with his rather powerful machinery of publicity on the top floor of Stearns Brothers' dry goods house was to keep the engines going and wait. Then, on the last day of the session of 1915, without any pre-liminary warning, Senator Coolidge walked into Stearns's office, pulled from his pocket a little slip of paper, put it on Stearns's desk, turned around, paced out with the sprightly, almost ladylike gait that comports with his silent manner, closed the door and was gone.   Stearns opened the paper, which read:

I am a candidate for lieutenant governor.

CALVIN COOLIDGE.

Then Stearns threw the belt onto the engine, and started his publicity campaign. He had access to many newspapers in many Massachusetts cities and knew many Massachusetts editors. So that the Coolidge campaign was well under way before Coolidge's opponents in the primary had time to start. And the lesson which earnest, ambitious American youth should learn from this fable is to go to college and to pick as their alma mater some institution which has harbored an alumnus in the advertising business.

It may be well here to pause and take a political survey of the convictions of Calvin Coolidge.   It may be assumed that when he wrote anything at that time, or at any time, what he wrote represented his honest conviction at that time. He has displayed obvious faults, but highfaluting promises to catch votes were not in the catalogue of his shortcomings. He wrote the state Republican platform in Massachusetts about this time and set forth the following pledges for his party; pledges which afterward were in the main redeemed. He helped to redeem them. The platform pledged the Republican Party to:

"The continued support of every means of compulsory and public education, cultural, vocational and technical, merited

retiring pensions, aid to dependent mothers, healthful hous-
ing and fair protection, reasonable hours and conditions of
labor, and the amplest protection for public health, work-
ingmen's compensation and its extension to intra-state railroads; official investigation of the price of necessities, pure
food with honest weights and measures; homestead commissions, city planning, the highest care and efficiency in the
administration of all hospital and penal institutions, proba-
tion and parole, care and protection of children and the
mentally defective; rural development, urban sanitation, state
and national conservation and reclamation; and every other
public means for social welfare consistent with the sturdy
character and resolute spirit of an understanding, self-sup-
porting, self-governing free people."

That was nearly ten years before he came to the
White House—a radical program for those days.
If Calvin Coolidge had appeared before Congress
in 1925 with a program as far in advance of
the times as that program was in advance of
1914, the accredited Republican leaders of Congress
would have jumped through the capitol windows to
get out of the presence of a Red; the Massachusetts
delegation taking the sash along! So do times
change and we change with them.

The candidacy of Coolidge for lieutenant governor was his first definite entrance into state-wide
popular acclaim. He has passed out of the Northampton cosmos into a larger world, and we must
always keep in our minds one important fact about
this man. He had been serving the public as councilman, representative, mayor and state senator

almost continuously for sixteen years. His total salary in all that time was less than $10,000. Of course, he had his law practice, which was a small practice in a small town. But he had sought no rich clients as a result of his public service, and rich clients do not come unsought to a rather ordinary lawyer who is rather over-nice about his honesty. So when Coolidge took wing from the Northampton nest to fly in a large field he was forty-two years old, had a wife and two young sons, was paying $27 a month as rent of a duplex semi-detached house, had a two-room office in the Masonic Temple in a not particularly favored part of the main street of Northampton, and probably was not earning all told more than $2,500 a year. Four years later, in Chicago, members of the Massachusetts delegation who were erroneously supposed to be supporting Coolidge as the Republican nominee for President, would take other delegates into a corner and say: "Well, I'll tell you what kind of a man Coolidge is. He is the kind of man who ran for lieutenant governor of Massachusetts because he needed the salary"!

The salary of lieutenant governor in Massachusetts was $2,000. The delegates who scandalized thus their candidate for the Presidency there at Chicago in 1920 are not to be blamed much, however deeply they wronged their fellow statesman. In politics, unless one produces evidence to the contrary, one is judged by outer signs. Coolidge, in all these years of public life, had given no outward and visible sign of any great inward and spiritual grace, had exhibited no peculiarly high patriotic motives, had paraded no noble aspirations, voiced no high ideals. He only accumulated political power. This negative attitude was part of some devilish complex in his heart, some deep inhibition that made him run away and hide as a little boy when company came, that made him stand battling before the kitchen door when strangers were inside before he would enter. Some complex, deep-seated and inexorable, kept him always with his worst foot forward, with his visions unguessed, with his heart screened and shielded, unresponsive, even in times of struggle and stress. One who studies him carefully is forced to the conclusion that here was an affectionate and aspiring man terribly repressed. Whether the repression was the natural environmental heritage of a hard, skimped Vermont family life, whether it followed somewhat the blows of death which rained upon his life in childhood, no one knows. But the repression is there, and the battle before the kitchen door probably goes on forever in Coolidge's life.

It must have been miserably hard for him to stand before audiences of strangers in the campaign of 1916 when they elected him lieutenant governor. But there he stood, a thin, timid, rasping-voiced Yankee, chipped out of the Vermont quarries, flinty and unyielding, speaking his piece. The papers very truly said this man is a "frost" as a public speaker. His colleague on the Republican ticket, Congressman Samuel McCall, who was running for governor that year, was one of the best vote-getters in New England. He had been drafted from Congress rather against his will to defeat David I. Walsh, a popular Democrat. McCall could fill any hall in Massachusetts by the power and charm of his name. Coolidge could empty any hall in Massachusetts in the same campaign by the graceless manner of his public appearance, yet McCall carried the state by only 6,000 and Coolidge won as lieutenant governor by nearly 50,000. He who had been a vote-getter in Northampton began to be a vote-getter in Massachusetts.

No one knows why. But there must be some channel of communication between this lanky and angular soul and the hearts of the American people. A reporter who saw Coolidge in that day says:

"It was as good as a show to watch him cross Tremont Street. The traffic was thick, of course, and sometimes Coolidge came to the street before the traffic cop was out in the morning. He always stopped, glanced, birdlike, up and down the street, measured the distance to the nearest car, and if he thought he could make it, he started across. If that car brushed his coat tails, he would not run. He had calculated the distance and the time. He had faith in his calculation. And evidently he considered it the driver's fault if he went faster than the Coolidge calculation provided. Having escaped, he did not exult. He never emotionalized. It was one of his few self-praising aphorisms that 'the Coolidges never slop over'! Presiding over the state senate, he sat and saw his pet measures triumph by one scary doubtful vote, or go down suddenly by a miserable mischance, and never did he flush or pale. He cared—he cared a lot. But wild Indians could not have tortured a groan or a grin from him. It seemed to be a part of some proud family tradition, to stoicize. He had just one vanity, as we reporters saw him in Boston. It was his writing. Men said Marvin, of the Home Markets League, later of the tariff board, wrote Coolidge's tariff speeches. He did not. Coolidge was too sure of himself ever to ask help in that direction; but anywhere else—yes, if he needed help. He had no other vanities."

Some way, something passed between Coolidge and the people of any given unit—a district, a town, a county, or a state—which brought confidence and respect from him to them. Of course, myths have aided him, but myths also have hampered him. The myth of the superman and the myth of the superstick probably have battled in the upper currents of popular imagination in a never-ending draw. But the real Coolidge, a conscientious, hard-working, hard-headed man of average intelligence which functions not intuitively, but in slow, logical processes which arrive at what we call common sense, not a brilliant nor highly valuable sense in crises— this real Coolidge has projected itself a real person into the hearts of the people when they wanted exactly that sort of a man. New England always seems to be wanting that sort of a man in this generation. New England statesmen for the past twenty years upon the whole have been men of intelligence rather than emotion, guided by conservative conscience rather than by large visions.

"Thin soil, highly cultivated" was the tag that Speaker Thomas B. Reed,—himself the last of the colorful statesmen of New England, successor of Sumner and Webster and the elder Adamses,—put on Henry Cabot Lodge. The surface soil of Coolidge is obviously thin, but under the rocks may be alluvial richness. If this richness had developed in his life, New England would have rejected him in this generation.

As Coolidge in a latter day impressed himself upon the map of the United States, so he impressed himself upon the map of Massachusetts in the campaign of 1916. Massachusetts, in the middle of the second decade of this century, when Coolidge first became a figure of state-wide interest, was in a turmoil of conflicting emotions. The Atlantic seaboard being frightened by the German menace, desired war as a protective measure, and yet being Irish in a considerable minority, was bitterly opposed to war in behalf of England. Also Massachusetts was a liberal state, and had certain yearnings, rather vague but far from negligible, for the Wilsonian liberalism. Into this turmoil came the Coolidge candidacy for lieutenant governor. He was a regular Republican with a liberal record, but had so little to say about his record that he frightened no conservatives. He talked economy, industry, caution and common sense, whatever that might mean at

the moment. And so he fitted into the acrostic of
the passing hour. A frugal people, who were making money enough to love industry for its own sake
just then, and who were too cautious and too Irish
to let the war spirit overcome them, voted for him.
Coolidge planned no campaign. His Vermont blood
won that election.

McCall may have been too rich. Coolidge, a poor
man, epitomized the time and the place, captured
the populace of his state. He ran true to form.
He had won thirteen elections, as councilman, city
solicitor, legislator, mayor and senator, always
reëlected, sometimes thrice elected, always gripping
something in the hearts of his fellow citizens. He
was lucky only in his opportunity to prove by an
endorsement at the polls that he had no luck, but
instead deep in the burred oak of his hard exterior, grew some instinct for the popular heart.
Hence we observe definitely in 1916 the arrival of
—the vote-getter.

CHAPTER IX

THE ESCAPE FROM NORTHAMPTON

Now, in most American states and in all Western states, the job of lieutenant governor is a son-in-law job, largely honorary, sometimes in line of promotion to the governorship, but generally about as important as the presidency of the Country Club in an inland city. In Massachusetts, however, the lieutenant governor is a part of the administrative end of the state government. He sits on a number of important executive boards. It is his duty to supervise and approve all expenditures of state money, to visit state institutions and to act with the governor's council upon gubernatorial appointments. The duties may be perfunctory, but Coolidge never made anything perfunctory. As he attended class meetings in Amherst punctiliously, followed the trivial proceedings carefully and finally came out of the background of his class, as he attended scrupulously every meeting of his party committee in Northampton and got acquainted with the wires of politics and came to know the men who pulled the wires— finally becoming city chairman—as he went to all the meetings of his legislative committees in the

assembly and senate—finally becoming president of
the senate—so he went into his work as lieutenant
governor with infinite pains and a heavy sense of
obligation. Coolidge's sense of obligation makes
him the New England conscience in trousers. In
the executive council he always stood by the governor. He was regular but not contentious. He
created no faction in the gubernatorial council, but
sat in quietly. Probably if there had been in the
politics of Massachusetts any tendency toward graft
or extravagance, he would have been the skeleton
at the feast who would have discouraged it by his
mere presence—the incarnate Puritan. The state
government of Massachusetts has a tradition for
honesty, a general trend toward economy, whatever
the municipal government of Boston may be. Coolidge's political beginnings in Northampton and all
his environment in Massachusetts were essentially
decent, essentially high-minded; moreover, the constitution and the laws of Massachusetts are liberal
to the point of national leadership. Massachusetts
enjoys the initiative and referendum. Massachusetts
controls her public utilities rigorously and scientifi-
cally. Massachusetts has a body of liberal legislation that compares favorably with that of any
other American state, "including the Scandinavian"
in La Follette's neighborhood. When Calvin Coolidge sat down with the executive council of the state
of Massachusetts to consider bills and to examine
the conduct of the state institutions, as lieutenant

governor, he was continuing a liberal education in a fairly liberal government. Certainly he was not becoming case-hardened as he would have become in a similar position in many another American state.

It may be noted rather definitely here that he was inspired by an ambition in these days of the lieutenant governorship for higher things. Being human, he needed no prod for his ambition. Nevertheless, he had it in Frank Stearns. Stearns had been able to help Coolidge considerably in his first state campaign for the primary nomination. Stearns was of service to Coolidge with his publicity machinery in his campaign for the election. But Stearns probably never was vital to Coolidge. Yet from 1915 Stearns became Coolidge's devoted monitor; also the tireless broker and promoter of the Coolidge fame. Also Stearns aspired more definitely than Coolidge himself for Coolidge's advancement. Stearns had no repressions in exhibiting his affection for Coolidge, nor did he ever flag in his tireless devotion to the Coolidge fortunes. They made an odd pair, this solid Boston merchant; a quiet, kindly, gentle-spoken man with a gift for publicity for others but no liking for it himself, and the young man with the tomblike silence and the poker face and the hard, resonant, nasal voice, poor as Job's turkey and proud as Lucifer, carrying somewhere about within him the burning but banked fires of an ambition for public service, not for his own sake but for the public good as he saw it—a real patriot right out of the fourth-reader stories and alas, perhaps, sometimes liable to fourth-reader limitations. Sancho Panza and Don Quixote reincarnated in New England would have made something such a pair as Stearns and Coolidge. The puzzle in this relation, indeed, the puzzle in the whole Coolidge career, is how far his sense of humor is suppressed. It flashes out, never for more than a second or two, occasionally in some witty saying, or in some sardonic action unexplained except that it is a humorous protest against grotesque wrongs. But if the Coolidge humor is at all dominant in his heart one cannot see how he could have moved through his career without getting himself in perspective and frivoling once in a while at his own solemn status in a topsy-turvy world. But he rarely frivols.

At the end of his first term as lieutenant governor he ran for reëlection. He won the nomination by nearly 85,000 plurality. The war was coming on. The nation was organizing for what at that moment it deemed its great abnegation. In Massachusetts Lieutenant Governor Coolidge added to his duty work upon the Committee of Public Safety. When we entered the war, Coolidge became more and more drawn into war activities and there, in the same earnest, silent way sat upon committees, influenced them somewhat through the mere negation of his presence somewhat affirmatively and became a force in the state, one of the political leaders of Massachusetts. He was more than a cog; he became a generator of power in the Murray Crane machine. He was elected for his second term for lieutenant governor by over 100,000 plurality: The vote-getter inexplicable!   An indifferent speaker, a social cipher, without financial resources and curiously needing little enough financial backing for all of Frank Stearns's ardor, he rose in Massachusetts steadily with a certain mysterious inexorableness which confounded politicians at the time and still baffles them. If one considers him only for what he seems, there is no answer to the Coolidge enigma.   But in Massachusetts, as in Northampton and as in Amherst, we find exactly the same story.   Always has he repeated himself.   He came into any situation colorless, unknown, insignificant.   He remained outwardly exactly the same figure that he entered, but by some inner appeal, some spiritual touch not of the material world, men come to recognize in him dependable qualities, profound spiritual agreements which begot first mere confidence, then blind enthusiasm.   And finally, because on the face of it, the Coolidge enthusiasm seemed absurd, his followers have built up the super-Coolidge myth to meet the minus-Coolidge myth which his enemies have created.   So the noble, brave, unerring super-Coolidge went out and fought with the dull, timid nonentity guided by the devilish imp of the Coolidge luck.

Always Coolidge has been too gentle to laugh at his enemies and too serious to laugh at himself. Probably if he began laughing at himself he would shatter the structure of his career. For no other career in modern American politics has been erected upon such fine strands, hanging by such delicate cables, as that eerie structure which supports the Coolidge career.

In 1919, by the grace of fortune and the help of Frank Stearns, together with his own mysterious potence as a vote-getter, Calvin Coolidge was elected governor of Massachusetts by a substantial majority. He still stopped at the Adams House, still kept his inside room there, still brought Mrs. Coolidge there when she was needed and still held his home in the semi-detached house on Massasoit Street in Northampton, where Mrs. Coolidge did her own work, looked after her own family, did her own part in the women's work of Northampton and continued to be a splendid symbol of the best type of middle-class American woman. And how Back Bay in Boston scorned it all, all that the Coolidges stood for; the Adams House, the $27-a-month home, the frugal ways, the day coach from Boston to Northampton, the solitary stogy, the parsimony of language, the whole resurrection of the Puritan type upon which 300 years ago Back Bay was founded and from which it sprang. It was as though Coolidge was the reincarnated poor relation of Back Bay, forever appearing to mock and humiliate it. He was a peace governor, elected when the reaction from war was beginning. There again the crossword puzzle of Coolidge's character fitted into the squares griddled upon the American heart. The people were cautious. They were voiceless. They were conscientiously trying to find some meaning from the peace, to make some poor salvage from the war, chiefly of material gain since the spiritual profit seemed to have vanished.

In Massachusetts the man who had been a rather prominent if silent figure on the war boards as lieutenant governor, who stood chiefly for economy and honesty, fitted into the sutures of popular imagination. He made a good governor but he did not change the curve of his life. He was a good state housekeeper, never a brilliant statesman. He revealed himself as a mild progressive, in the declining days of the progressive cult and then loomed into national prominence through the Boston police strike. Reference to that strike projects the narrative a few months forward, yet it must be considered here.

For the Boston police strike furnishes the accidental element in the Coolidge career. Some such fortuitous circumstance is thrust into every life for good or evil. Yet without those circumstances and in spite of them our lives would be in many ways what they are—essentially, deeply and in the end. The selections of the undefinable motive of life that we call destiny, are baffling. Coolidge would have been the same Coolidge to the end of his life without the Boston police strike; but without it, what would America have been? How much did destiny need Coolidge? How would America have found just such another perfect epitome of her mood, and the world so exact an interpreter of the fear impulse which enmeshed mankind in the first half of the third decade of this century, without the Boston police strike that discovered Calvin Coolidge to his countrymen? For forty-four years life had been making out of New England blood and background the cautious, intelligent, courageous, conscientious, conservative Yankee. He was in that spring of 1919 a most commonplace man, in appearance, in career, in aspiration. "There is nothing to him," declared the casual appraising verdict of his contemporaries.

For fifty years his country had been enjoying a boom—fundamentally spiritual, but externally most substantial. Adventure after adventure had come to the land. A desert from the Mississippi River to the Pacific Coast had been made to blossom as a rose. A mighty commerce had been erected in the United States. East of the Mississippi an agricultural people had turned definitely to industry. A battling but still more or less festive excursion into social and industrial justice had engaged the people's politics, and exalted their hearts. They were drunk with hope. Bryan, Roosevelt, La Follette, and finally Wilson had stimulated their idealism, had intoxicated the people with a faith in the millennium. Then came the war. Then, alas! came the debacle of faith—and the cold gray dawn of reality. The world was sick of millennial promises, would have none of its Messiahs! America tried Harding, and death came in mercy and took him away. How did his countrymen find Coolidge? How did they have him in the wings awaiting his cue—exactly his kind; exactly the man of the zero hour. Was the Boston police strike an accident—or was Coolidge the accident? Or perhaps the whole crash of human hopes that shook the world at Versailles was the accident. But how did they all fit together in one piece of destiny that affected the direction and force of the thing we like to call progress in the affairs of man?

CHAPTER X

THE SPOTLIGHT FINDS OUR HERO

Until September, 1919, Calvin Coolidge was a local politician with no fame beyond the boundaries of Massachusetts. His record as governor was the ordinary record of the ordinary governor of the ordinary state. It was an honest record of a capable man rather above the average in intelligence, who made few mistakes somewhat because he was chary of taking any action. The contemporary governor of Maine, Vermont, or Connecticut might as well have aspired to the Presidency as Calvin Coolidge, who probably did not even remotely aspire to the Presidency in that day.

During the summer of 1919, labor troubles were annoying the business world. A national strike of maintenance-of-way men was threatened in the spring. In Europe the Allies were spending much time and treasure in a vain attempt to overthrow the Bolsheviks. President Wilson had come home from Europe with his unhappy treaty and covenant, bound in one document and doomed in one document. Bela Kun sat a sinister figure at the head of the government in Hungary. A strike riot occurred at Hammond, Indiana, and the high cost of living was disorganizing orderly, economic life all over the country. Labor was asking for a tripartite operation of the American railroads known as the Plumb plan, which seemed to American business men as menacing as the constitution of Lenine and Trotzky in Moscow. The sugar shortage and the fortunes that were piling up as a result of that shortage were undermining American confidence and making unrest. The newspaper headlines of the early days of September, 1919, were filled with these things, which in turn filled the hearts of the people with fear and dread of some uncertain visitation which might wreck their little world.

One fine morning early in September Calvin Coolidge, governor of Massachusetts, walked across the Common to his office from the Adams House to find on his desk notes on a possible police strike in Boston. The American Federation of Labor had been organizing the Boston police. The mayor of Boston had denied the right of the policemen to organize, claiming that the policeman's relations with society was not that of a workman but of a guardian. Nineteen policemen had been tried, found guilty, and dismissed for joining the American Federation Union. Mr. Samuel Gompers, head of the Federation, seemed to be encouraging the strike. It was not a strike called upon the question of wages, but on the question of the rights of policemen to join a union in affiliation with the American Federation of Labor. Technically, the strike was called because those nineteen policemen were dismissed from the service, having been found guilty by a nonpartisan city committee. They were convicted of agitating for the labor union in opposition to the explicit orders of the police commissioner. Now this police commissioner was a state official, not a city official, appointed by Governor Coolidge's predecessor in office. To a certain extent he was under state supervision if not control in the administration of the police affairs of Boston. The mayor of Boston felt that a large number of the police officers would go out in the threatened strike. Apparently the police commissioner did not share the mayor's fears and probably the police commissioner, reporting to the governor, gave him a confidence in the situation which was not warranted by the facts. There matters stood when the strike was called Tuesday evening, September 9, 1919. More than a thousand policemen left their posts. Rioting began about midnight and continued until Wednesday morning when the mayor called out the militia within the city of Boston, a power which he exercised legally. But Boston was in panic. The police commissioner under the state government informed the mayor that conditions justified the mayor's action. Those two were in agreement. That agreement did not allay the panic of Boston. Boston wanted all the troops in the state. The governor sent word that the adjutant general was prepared to execute any request

for troops made under the law. Hysteria spread
from Boston to its suburbs. Later in the day the
mayor called upon the governor for three regiments
from outside the city, which the governor sent.

Wednesday passed. Massachusetts began to feel
the terror that gripped Boston. By Thursday morning the mayor's committee, a widely representative
committee of intelligent Bostonians fully informed
about the strike, reported "that order had been generally restored in the city." The committee's report
did not calm the city, nor allay the fear of the state.

But the governor did not show the least sign of
perturbation. Neither did he relax his attention.
He kept the adjutant general with him day and
night. The governor made it clear but not dramatically emphatic—Coolidge never is dramatic—that
he was supporting the police commissioner who was
the only official actually connected with the state
administration under the law. The tension was
increased Thursday when a delegation of labor leaders representing men working upon the important
industries in the city of Boston and the adjoining
towns—public utilities affecting food and transpor-
tation by land and water—called upon the governor
and threatened a general strike in eastern Massachusetts. The governor heard them. The governor
told them that he would support the police commissioner, a cryptic statement, and then stood
dumbly before the delegation in a long silence until
the labor leaders had left the room. Red headlines

predicting anarchy blazed in a dozen newspapers. All New England stood aghast. Coolidge made no sign of his intention. Later, when told that labor unions all over eastern Massachusetts were voting almost unanimously for a general strike, he paused and said, undramatically:

"We will meet that situation when we have to."

New England was almost hysterical. Letters and telegrams came in a flood to the governor's desk demanding action. The governor did not act. He was as parsimonious of action as he was of words. Two wild days had passed in which Boston papers and Boston public men were clamoring for action. A general strike, if it had occurred, would have precipitated anarchy. Governor Coolidge stood before that threat as he walked before the whizzing cars in the Tremont Street traffic—unhurried—waiting perhaps; perhaps hoping that time would help him; certainly not adding to the excitement of the hour by threats, promises or by the hokum of tragic gestures. A stone image would have viewed the impending calamity with the same composure. Was his attitude the reflex of restraint or spiritual calm or indifference?

No one knows. Thursday night he called out the whole state guard. The strike was broken. And so Coolidge backed crabbedly into the spotlight. It was typically Coolidgesque, undramatic almost to the point of unimportance. He was justified by history undoubtedly in his long delay. If one would

accuse Coolidge of not acting in any situation until
he had to act, he would reply, "Well, why should I?"

"Hello, Chatterbox," said General Edwards to
Coolidge one fine day in Washington.

"Well," Coolidge drawled, "what I don't say
doesn't get me into as much trouble as what you do
say."

This is the golden rule of Coolidge: Economy—
economy of words, economy of action, which never
by any chance may be called laziness and surely is
not the result of economy of thought. Probably
this spiritual serenity does not cloak a lack of imagination. It is old New England, cautious, conservative, still courageous but not excited about its
courage; a throwback into another century; a queer
apparition in the modern world. And this decent,
orderly, well-considered action, thoroughly dedra-
matized by a man who never made a pose in his life,
threw Calvin Coolidge upon the national stage, a
national figure as he had come up from Northampton to Boston a state figure.

He must have known that he was a national figure
from the days of the Boston police strike. He could
not have read the papers the week after the settlement of the strike without seeing his name mentioned for the Presidency. The day he called out
the full state militia Boston would have crowned
him king, yet he went to his inside room in the
Adams House, one of the cheaper rooms of the
hotel, and closeted himself there that night invisible

to reporters, studying some state problem. Then
he went home to Northampton, still avoiding the
limelight.

An old friend wrote him a joyous letter of con-
gratulation, one among the thousands which he
received. He answered it:

Dear Newt:

I am glad you liked what I did about the police strike.
I thought you would.

Yours truly,

CAL.

It takes a genius to quack like that with his pen.
Yet the fact that he signed himself Cal to an old
friend shows the human desire for human associa-
tion, affection, comradeship, which the man inside
his shell some way belies. He was Cal to thousands; Cal always in Plymouth, generally Cal or
"Red" in Ludlow, frequently Cal in Northampton
and sometimes in Boston—Cal to his face always
among old friends, sometimes among new ones, yet
a sort of reserved and respected Cal who never in
his life was slapped on his back.

When he burst into national fame after the police
strike and for a few months functioned for the first
time as a hero he changed neither his friends nor
his ways. The faithful Frank Stearns and a few
Amherst men started out to capitalize the heroship
with a Presidential boom. They opened offices in
Washington. By Coolidge's orders the offices were
promptly closed. He refused rather stubbornly to

talk about his Presidential aspirations to Boston reporters, genially snarling something about his duties as governor being paramount. In many another man this attitude would have seemed a rather infelicitous gesture of self-righteousness, complicated with a sneaking and hypocritical desire for advertising. But the gesture was most sincere. It is hard to explain to a sophisticated generation how the gesture could be sincere, but it was. As one goes into the Coolidge career carefully, one senses, and even his enemies were compelled to grant to him, a certain unemotional honesty, the more substantial because it was cold. This honesty was a first premise of most of his actions. Not that he was perfect. He sometimes blundered. He was limited in his outlook, sometimes sadly was cramped in his vision. He had no quality of daring that makes a great leader, however brave he was. But he was square with himself, even as a hero. He was canonized by the forces that made a saint of Grover Cleveland for putting down the Debs strike thirty-one years before. The babble of the crowd did not drive him mad, as it might have unbalanced a lighter man. Maybe he knew his own heart's weakness in the time of trial; at least he was a man in the hour when the mob jabbered its hosannas at him. It must always be said to the credit of Calvin Coolidge that in his big moment, when fame first touched him, he kept his faith; he refused to be the demagogue of a plutocracy which his heart approved.

His heroship lay not in the fact that he called out the troops and saved his state from anarchy. It lay in the fact that having called out the troops, having heard the acclaim of the multitude, he turned to his humdrum routine of the day, and refused to allow his name to go on the primary ballots in Massachusetts as a candidate for the Presidency.

PART III

CINDERELLA AT A GAY PARTY

CHAPTER XI

MASSACHUSETTS GETS A SURPRISE

At the Republican National Convention of 1920, the Massachusetts delegation formally presented the name of Governor Calvin Coolidge as a candidate for the Presidency. The presentation was perfunctory. The delegation from Massachusetts was only morganatically attached to Coolidge. The evident distaste of the Massachusetts delegation for their governor was explained variously. Some said that Senator Murray Crane was sick. Others said that the Massachusetts delegates regarded the aspirations of Coolidge's friends, notably Frank Stearns and some Holyoke paper makers, as preposterous. The semi-detached house and the quite detached honesty of Coolidge, his high-and-mightiness in closing the Washington headquarters opened to promote his candidacy, his decent refusal to go into the Massachusetts Presidential primary, had aroused the contempt of certain Massachusetts statesmen. A few Massachusetts delegates were genuinely with Coolidge, but with the divided delegation he faded out of the Presidential picture. The powerful under-currents of our national life swept

aside the Coolidge Presidential candidacy and took
hold of the candidacy of Warren G. Harding, of
Ohio. Harding was the complete antithesis of Wilson, and the currents of that day were anti-Wilson.
If Coolidge himself was disappointed at the failure
of the National Republican Convention seriously to
consider his name as a Presidential candidate he
made no show of it during the three days of the
balloting. At four o'clock, Saturday afternoon, the
fifth day of the Republican National Convention,
Harding was nominated for the Presidency by a
cabal of United States senators who controlled the
convention. A telegram, early in the afternoon
when Harding's victory was assured, told Coolidge
that he would be considered as a candidate for Vice-
President. An odd candidacy it was, and a weird
little campaign, which landed Calvin Coolidge in
the Vice-Presidency.

It is hard to unravel events and to find among the
cords that draw circumstances into place, what cord
is the core of the cable. The nomination of Coolidge for Vice-President was drawn inevitably from
a vision into reality by a curious skein of fate. The
most visible string was in the hand of Frank Stearns,
the Fidus Achates of the Coolidge destiny. Frank
Stearns was of course one of the few faithful hearts
in the Massachusetts delegation of 1920. Four
years before, in 1916, while Coolidge was still state
senator, Frank Stearns had appeared at the Chicago
convention, a lonely and prophetic figure, the butt

of ribald merriment among the Massachusetts delegation, canvassing for State Senator Coolidge as a Presidential candidate. Even Murray Crane, who was at the moment using Coolidge as a good cogwheel in his machine, saw the humor of this, and the Northampton crowd in the delegation shook with glee at Stearns's devotion. Stearns and two or three other Amherst men had printed during the latter part of 1919 and the early part of 1920 seventy thousand copies of a book called "Have Faith in Massachusetts," made up of the speeches and official addresses delivered by Calvin Coolidge at various stages of his early career but chiefly during his term as lieutenant governor. This book was sent broadcast over the country to every important leader of public opinion in the Republican party; editors, governor, congressmen, state senators, national committeemen, state committeemen, possible delegates to the convention and actual delegates to the convention as the spring of 1920 developed them. Some of these books were read; possibly ten thousand out of the seventy thousand. They were the seed that fell on good ground. Now these 10,000 readers were convinced that Coolidge was a sane, conservative and obviously conscientious man without pose or affectation. They created a popularity for him not deep but wide that covered the land. The Boston police strike had created a mythical character, a strong, silent, indomitable creature who had dramatically saved New England from anarchy

and had put labor unions in what the popular mind
of the day deemed their proper place.

For at that moment labor unions were in bad
odor. The soldiers coming home from the World
War felt that the unions had made it possible for
labor to profiteer during the war. The high scale
of wages, in spite of the high prices of commodities,
was taking something substantial out of profits and
certainly was taking a deep, cruel bite out of the fixed
incomes of millions of worthy people. This helped
to make Calvin Coolidge, the man who had curbed
the labor unions, a popular figure in that middle-
class stratum which dominates the Republican
Party. All this was not in the least accidental. The
citizens in that stratum, not understanding Coolidge,
made the mythical Coolidge. His soul, like the soul
of old John Brown, the marcher, entered the Republican convention of 1920.

Now delegates to a convention, particularly to
a Republican convention, are like soldiers under
orders. The delegates to that Republican convention of 1920 were under the control of the Republican United States senators from the various states
—the Senate oligarchy of the period. These senators had no place for Coolidge in their cosmos.
They would have taken Lowden; or indeed might
have taken Wood under compulsion. Harding was
their hearts' desire. He was one of them. He had
no obstreperous courage, no inhibiting cautions about
taking the Senate program and in addition to all

this the Senate knew him as a good fellow. He
liked a good story and was not squeamish about
its flavor. He played the senatorial poker games
and took an occasional nip in the senatorial locker
room. To top all that he was a Republican of an
old school after their own heart. So when Wood,
crushing Lowden, spent his own strength, orders
came from the Senate oligarchy, variously veiled,
to the delegates to take Harding. The Coolidge candidacy surely was in their hearts, but orders were
orders. Obedience is the first law of party regularity and there was no irregularity in that convention. A prolonged deadlock might have produced Coolidge as a candidate. But at the close
of the fourth day of the convention—the second day
of the voting—Harding won.

The convention did not adjourn after the nomination of Harding, but proceeded to name a Vice-
President. The convention had obeyed orders in
the matter of the Presidential nomination, but a
wild, free moment followed.

When Harding was nominated, the Massachusetts
delegation began to disintegrate. They felt—at
least many of them felt—that Coolidge had gone
far enough politically. A dozen members of the
Massachusetts delegation went to their hotels. The
Vice-Presidency at a Presidential convention is a
consolation prize. Its dramatics are unimportant.
The Massachusetts delegates who went to their
hotels were the old stagers, sure that nothing else

interesting would happen. They were right. All
that happened came quite casually. The pegs were
set for the nomination of Senator Lenroot of Wis-
consin for Vice-President. The senatorial group
which controlled the convention, which easily nominated Harding, had told Henry Allen, governor of
Kansas, that he could not have the Vice-Presidential
nomination, because of his fight with labor upon the
Kansas industrial court. The Senate group was
enthroned. It announced that it would have no
labor baiter on the ticket—not dreaming of Coolidge and the Boston strike!

But the thing that happened in the Massachusetts
delegation happened in a number of delegations; all
the old stagers left the hall. When the order of the
day for Vice-Presidential nominations came, Lenroot's name was properly presented by Senator
Medill McCormick. Massachusetts knew the senatorial program. So Coolidge's name as a Vice-
Presidential candidate was not presented by Massachusetts. The New Englanders were all taking the
senatorial program.

But as the dull hour passed for nominating by
courtesy various candidates for the Vice-Presidency,
in the Oregon delegation a school-reader patriot,
who took the convention and the Republican Party
and his own idea of America seriously, climbed on
a chair and began speaking. No one heard what he
was saying in the din. No one cared to hear. He
clamored for recognition. The chairman of the con-

vention tried to restore order. The gavel created a second's silence. In that second the Oregon patriot bawled out the name of "Coolidge," while in the general pandemonium which followed he made a speech which no one heard.

But the name struck fire. The national Republican heart responded. Every delegate to the convention had received from Frank Stearns a book containing the Coolidge speeches, and every delegate who was not an old stager had read the speeches. The old stagers went to headquarters for their pabulum. But alas! They went to their hotels after the big battle was over. So when the Oregonian bawled Coolidge's name from his chair, in that second of silence the patriots rallied to the call. Before the balloting was half through, the senatorial group was appalled to see Lenroot's chances waning. "No one but a fool would have nominated Coolidge," they said of the Oregonian. Then by way of comment and consolation, they added: "A fool for luck!" And so it was.

And having got to their hotels, the Massachusetts statesmen heard the shocking news that the convention of its own motion had broken out of bounds and had nominated Calvin Coolidge for Vice-President. Wearily the Massachusetts statesmen began cursing the Coolidge luck.

In Boston rather lonesomely outside the situation, as remote as the old stagers of the Massachusetts delegation, sat Coolidge in his little inside room at the Adams House with Mrs. Coolidge and a faithful friend or so waiting for the news of the ballot. Mrs. Coolidge kept the talk going for an hour. The telephone rang. Coolidge took the message, looking down his nose abjectly as he always does in his great moments! He put up the receiver and snapped out one word:

"Nominated."

Now Coolidge squared with something in the hearts of the delegates. His qualities answered some yearning in their souls for a man of iron. Coolidge had faith in Massachusetts a long time before Massachusetts had much faith in Coolidge. The nomination of Calvin Coolidge for Vice-President in spite of the apathy of Massachusetts, came out of an instinctive feeling of the responsible, if not the recognized, leadership of the party all over America, choosing a man whose qualities matched something deeply implanted in the Republican heart. Embittered, envious or shallow cynics said it was cheap calling unto cheap; but after all, democracies are entitled to what they desire even if they are not always yearning for marble statues of heroic proportions! One test of a democracy comes in the answer to the question: Is the popular will obeyed? In the choice of Calvin Coolidge as a Vice-Presidential candidate of the dominant American party in 1920, the popular party will revolting from its leadership certainly expressed itself.

Let us consider those delegates that we may understand their hearts. The Republican Party in the generation since the Civil War has been the party of business. Its conventions are made up of business men, their professional servants and a few large farmers who in reality are agricultural manufacturers. The Republican Party has the master instinct strongly developed. It is the party of property, brightly camouflaged as "the party of prosperity." Quite incidentally it has certain vague and sometimes rather definite yearnings for justice; but after all, those yearnings are secondary to its desire for prosperity.

The delegates of 1920 were not confused by any Rooseveltian complexes which might have made cross-purposes in 1912 or even 1908 or 1904. They were bankers, merchants, lawyers, farmers, with a small sprinkling of members of the more learned professions, and what they most desired was honesty, industry, caution, sincerity and sanity. They hankered for all these chiefly because they were the necessary antecedents of stable prosperity. The war had rocked the world and a vast caution— a deadly fear in high places—was gripping the hearts of men. There sat in the convention a picked crowd of a thousand delegates coming straight from the heart of American business with no nonsense about them. Their inner aspirations fitted exactly the advertised characteristics of the man in the Coolidge myth, indeed, fitted also the characteristics of the man who was the real Coolidge. The nomination of Coolidge for Vice-President at Chicago in 1920 was as perfect an example of the working of the selective processes of American democracy functioning perfectly as our history presents. Democracy there functioned instinctively without recognized leadership and without authoritative direction.

When the politicians of the Republican National Committee took a look at their Vice-Presidential candidate in the early campaign of 1920 they were appalled. The man had never been out of New England; had never slept in a Pullman berth, knew no national politicians, had no sense of the country that comes from even New York or Washington contacts with the country and was as cold and as dumb as an oyster. As a popular speaker in the West the party managers felt that Coolidge would fail. They were correct in their feeling. Coolidge went to Minnesota and the crowd left his meeting. His reserved manner, the twang of his Yankee voice, the utter absence of oratorical frills in his speeches, his passionate determination not to play the hero, a determination which seemed to Republican statesmen of the hour like a mean denial of their game, gave the Republican campaign managers in 1920 a distaste for Coolidge which they hardly tried to conceal. At Republican national headquarters, lordly men of fame and gorgeous fallen angels of ill fame—the elder and defunct statesmen whom the Roosevelt era had annihilated—patronized, scandalously, the decent meek little Moses from Massachusetts whom the Fates left in the bullrushes at the Chicago convention.   These worthies of the Sanhedrin sent him campaigning in the South, talking to the hillmen of Tennessee and of Georgia, the unschooled poor white Appalachian cousins of the sturdy Green Mountain boys.   Possibly his presence in the hills of Tennessee had something to do with bringing Tennessee into the Republican column.   No one could say.   Coolidge's friends like to claim it. But he was surely shunted off the main traveled road of politics into these Southern by-paths in his campaign.   He was a by-word around the National Republican headquarters, the Cinderella of the Republican household.

CHAPTER XII

The election of 1920, which made Calvin Coolidge Vice-President, took to Washington the queerest political specimen ever elected to high office. Barrett Wendell, a high-caste Back-Bay Brahmin, described Coolidge in that day thus:

"A small, hatched-faced, colorless man, with a tight-shut, thin-lipped mouth; very chary of words, but with a gleam of understanding in his pretty keen eye."

President Harding called Vice-President Coolidge into the Cabinet meetings—perhaps through the prompting of some deep prescience. But never once in two years, except when some one asked a definite question of the Vice-President did Coolidge open his mouth at a Cabinet meeting. He sat listening—just as he sat in his freshman class meetings, in the Northampton Republican city committee, in the joint committee of the Massachusetts assembly, and again as lieutenant governor in the governor's council. He was developing an near-minded man. His capacity for absorbing details without question must have been taxed in those days. Yet he came out of

114

COOLIDGE AS VICE-PRESIDENT

Barrett Wendell, a high caste Back Bay Brahmin, described Coolidge in that day thus: "A small, hatchet-faced, colorless man, with a tight-shut, thin-lipped mouth; very chary of words, but with a gleam of understanding in his pretty keen eye." Note well the eye.

(Page 114)

the Cabinet sessions a well-equipped man for the job
Fate held in store for him.

Coolidge was no innocent. He could not have sat
in the Cabinet and in the Senate of the United States
for two years without sensing what was going on
under the Harding administration. No one could
frequent the White House in those days without
suspecting the Ohio crowd, surrounding Harding,
of much of the irregularity which afterward came
out of the Harding administration; which indeed
became matters of public scandal after Harding's
death. Probably few hints of the machinations of
the Ohio crowd came to the Cabinet. But some
sense of odor if not of stench must have penetrated
even there. Fall was there. Daugherty was there,
and Denby; the innocent but unlucky, each of whom
knew exactly what the other was doing. More than
their common knowledge, their common expressions
of self-righteous justification for their official orders,
rulings and actions must have breathed around the
Cabinet meetings some premonitory scent of what
soon was to fill the air of Washington with disgust-
ing accusations. Why then, one asks who admires
militant righteousness with a quick trigger, did not
Vice-President Coolidge act? Even as Vice-President, of course, Roosevelt would have acted upon
his suspicions; probably Wilson also would have
done something to create an alibi for himself against
a future day of wrath. But Coolidge is Coolidge.
His way is his way. To those who would question

his sincerity or courage a sufficient answer is found in an incident in the Senate while Vice-President Coolidge was presiding.

The Senate was in uproar. Senator McCumber and Senator Reed were yelling at each other, hurling large ragged words with more speed than control. Other senators were crying "order" and the galleries were standing to see the combatants clinch.

"Use your gavel! Use your gavel—restore order," pleaded the parliamentarian at the Vice-President's elbow.

Vice-President Coolidge sat calmly watching the fracas. Again the parliamentarian clamored for action. Turning to his monitor with solemn face, the Vice-President replied:

"Yes, I shall if they get excited!"

And he let the senators calm their own riot. The answer is found again if one watches him in the police strike, waiting serenely until the last possible moment before acting. If one watches him at every crisis of his career waiting to move until the dramatics of the act are gone and only the need to do something remains—his answer is, "Why sh'u'd I?"

The Coolidge alarm strikes at the zero hour! Sitting in the Cabinet meetings listening to the talk, watching the drift and tendency of things, with no legal authority to act, and with naturally a voracious appetite for silence, Vice-President Coolidge was not tempted to speak. But in the fullness of time he knew exactly how to act. As Vice-President he had

taken the measure of Fall, of Denby, of Daugherty.
The action came only when President Coolidge had
the power to act. It may have seemed futile to
those who desire a moral lesson, a striking folk-play
staged for the populace. But such action as finally
came sufficed, apparently, to carry confidence to the
people. The silent inaction of Coolidge in the
Harding Cabinet was perfectly in character. While
he was Vice-President, some friends were repeating
to him the strictures upon his action in the Boston
strike; explaining how his wisdom and his courage
were questioned by those who maintained that he
waited too long and who clamored viciously that he
was not responsible in the least for the final strike
settlement. After the friendly lodge of sorrow had
finished its ritual, Coolidge answered:

"Well, I believe I was governor at the time!"

If the man has a sense of his failure to meet the
histrionic demands of great occasions, he conceals
it. His temperament furnishes such salve as his
spirit needs to heal bruises of regret, if he has
regrets.

But the curious thing about the Coolidge career
is his weird way of repeating himself at every change
in his circumstances. There seems to be no free will
in his life. Environment, time and chance pass before and around him like a moving panorama. He
remains stationary, doing in various environments
at various times in varying fortunes always the same
thing. The deep essential spirit of the man produces

with life as X, over and over again the same equation.   He appears, is ignored, accepts neglect and
a certain added jibing, allows time to act upon his
associates, who gradually come to understand him,
then respect him.   Whereupon, without changing, he
goes right on performing his day's work, piles endeavor on endeavor, and comes to some place in his
life where he takes an upward jump.   He is boosted
by circumstances over which he has small control,
and finds that he has been preparing all along for
exactly the new place into which he is landed.   Then,
being a stranger at the new landing, he begins all
over to enact his meager dull little pantomime on the
larger stage.   Out of which dumb show he emerges
in due course a hero of a sort.   So it was with him
at Amherst, at Northampton, in the legislature, in
the state senate, in the governor's office, in the Vice-
Presidency.   Over and over he puppets his way
across the stage; scenes change, but the wires are
always in the same hands.   Fate's?   Or Coolidge's?
God only knows!

Coolidge himself does not reveal his own opinion.
Occasionally a story bobs up which indicates a certain satisfaction in the self-made man.   When he
and Mrs. Coolidge in their early married life were
at a gubernatorial reception, facetiously they tried
the governor's chair and were chased out.   Fifteen
years later, taking the chair officially, he said to
Mrs. Coolidge, not having mentioned in all the years
the former evacuation: "Well—they won't run us

out this time!" and never spoke of the matter again. But it must live in his heart, the sense that he has come a long and happy way, that he has climbed far and well. But to reveal his pride would be an emotional exhibition. So he is silent.

In those halcyon Vice-Presidential years, Calvin Coolidge dined every night he spent in Washington, generally at some official dinner, and sat silently through the meal, a sincerely appreciative eater, but not quite hearty. He seemed willing to lend the physical presence of his digestive apparatus, but not his personality, to the feast. His spirit he withheld in some deep abashment; though curiously he seemed to be enjoying himself back in his inner sanctum. Débutantes, tuft-hunting hostesses and various social babblers tried to tempt him to persiflage, and he snapped sharp monosyllables at them all. Quoth he to a voluble hostess sympathetically chattering about the Vice-President's hard lot in having to attend so many official dinners:

"Have to eat somewhere!"

And let that do for his evening's converse!

In the presiding officer's chair in the Senate, he was dry and crisp, methodical, conscientious and impersonal. He seemed to make no friends among the senators.

We have followed the career of Calvin Coolidge now far enough to consider him in relation to his enemies. The embarrassing part of a research for his enemies, is that he has made none. A number of people held him in low esteem. Doubtless he reciprocated their feelings. But there seemed to be in his books no black lists, no persons whom he held in fond and irretrievable loathing; contempt maybe, he had, but not active hate. For hate also is an emotion. In Massachusetts, Coolidge tried hard not to be a factionalist. But certain adherents of the late Senator Lodge seemed to delight in honoring Coolidge with their illy concealed scorn. In his gubernatorial activities Coolidge favored and actively promoted economies which separated a number of amiable patriots of the tax-eating variety from the state pay-roll. They built fires against the granite of his indifference and got their temperature up for their pains. The Lodge difference never amounted to a feud. Yet it stuck. Its root was in Back Bay and Beacon Street. It was hard for the hereditary rulers of Massachusetts to surrender to a newcomer, a Vermonter, an Amherst man, a social bound-boy, who did not even look for the red ears! It deeply saddened Back Bay to know that of a Sunday, Mrs. Coolidge, the governor's wife in Northampton, might possibly be helping to put the Sunday dinner on the table. But the governor, if he knew of the grief of Back Bay, ignored it. In all his career he has made few friends, lost none, and has cherished no enemies. Hating Coolidge is a sadly unresponsive business; kickless, stale and unprofitable.

As Vice-President, Calvin Coolidge revealed no

capacity or genius for his place. He trudged along doing the hour's work well and let each day be sufficient to its own evil. Apparently he sat there in the presiding officer's chair unimaginative, uninteresting, self-contained, laconic, automatic.

He went to Northampton when he could, lived in his little duplex house in the same simple way that he had lived as governor and as state senator and as mayor of his town. They raised the rent on him to $35 a month—a deep and grievous wrong! He and Mrs. Coolidge seemed happy there, normally resuming their Northampton ways. The Vice-President paced sedately down the streets of Northampton, attended to his small business affairs, was Cal to those who Cal'd him, and clearly nursed no lofty notion of his high destiny to keep him away from his old friends. The only change that Northampton noticed in him was that he had given up his solemn annual glass of beer, in deference to law and order. Whatever his aspirations were, whatever pride he had in his honored office, never appeared upon the surface of his life. His sons worked in their vacations; went up into Vermont for a job, worked in the tobacco fields at hard, back-bending work, but no harder than their father had worked, nor their grandfather nor their great-grandfathers before them. Mrs. Coolidge kept her own house with one maid, retained her pleasant contacts with Northampton and the two kept abreast of the local politics of town with the usual emotions of home folks

viewing the home spectacle. Smith College, voting
for a Democratic mayor, reduced the Republican
majority in Ward Two. Whereat in righteous
wrath Vice-President Coolidge wrote an article for
a women's magazine about the danger of the Reds
in our women's colleges, a perfect example of the
model country-town man reasoning from the particular to the universal.

He never has lost his country-town view of life,
never has been the world citizen; never will he be.
He has lived and will die, no matter where Fate
sends him, Cal Coolidge, of Northampton, of Ludlow and of Plymouth, the small-town American who
is more typical of America than our cosmopolitan
boulevardier. No boulevardier—Calvin Coolidge.
One flag, one country, one conscience, one wife, and
never more than three words will do him all his life.

In the summer of 1923 the Coolidges left Washington to spend the summer with Col. John Coolidge, the Vice-President's father in Plymouth, Vermont. President Harding was on his Western trip—
tired, but not broken, and the newspaper accounts
of the Presidential journey seemed to indicate that
President Harding was having a good time. Plymouth, Vermont, is a small dot on the map, three
or four houses, the Coolidge store, which Grandfather Coolidge sold a few years ago, the church,
and the cemetery, a house or two and a wide place
in the road leading up the hill to the schoolhouse.

That's all of it. Less than fifty farmers live in the village.

The Vice-President was helping his father with the hay crop; Mrs. Coolidge was resting and doing her share of the housework in the little cottage where the Coolidge family lived, and the two Coolidge youngsters, as true sons of a Yankee sire, were working in the fields for a near-by farmer. There was simple, middle-class country-town America, rusticating.

The evening papers of the day before came up to Plymouth from Ludlow every morning, and the morning papers were brought up later in the day. Not even a rural phone connected the Coolidges with the world at Ludlow, the nearest telegraph office. The papers brought the daily story of the President's journey to the Pacific Coast, to Alaska and back. Into the story came disquieting rumors of his illness. But evidently it was not a serious illness. He rallied, and the Coolidges, who never borrowed trouble, were not disturbed. They did the day's work happily. Living at a hotel in Washington rather modestly, they had been able to put by a little of the Vice-Presidential salary, and with reasonable hope of another nomination and election—five years more in the Vice-Presidency—they probably had dreams of owning their own home in Northampton and living as befitted the dignity of an ex-Vice-President of the United States. It was a peaceful world

—there in Plymouth that summer—but bright and happy.

July 29, 1923, the Coolidge family went to bed tired, after a hard day's work, and the lights of the coal-oil lamps in the village had winked out by ten o'clock. Just before midnight the silence of the place was broken by the chugging of an automobile. Col. John Coolidge, a light sleeper, awoke, went to the front door, and found a man with a message for his son, the Vice-President. The man could not keep the news for the Vice-President and told Col. John, who told his son. The message was from the secretary of the President in San Francisco announcing President Harding's sudden death. Another car came chugging down the road to Plymouth, and another and still another, all in a few moments. The flood of a new life was rushing in. From one end to the other of New England came reporters hurrying to the village. There at midnight for three hours Plymouth held the spotlight of the world.

Col. John was in his late seventies. Emotions could no longer stir him deeply. His son suppressed the outward signs of the tumult in his heart. But Calvin Coolidge's wife, Grace, grasped the truth. Also she got the terror of it, realized that a new, strange and maybe tragic period lay before her and those she loved. A surge of dread for she knew not what moved her to tears; while her husband, the stoic, picked out his best black suit and methodically dressed for the occasion.

PLYMOUTH, THE DAY AFTER PRESIDENT HARDING DIED

"The flood of a new life came rushing in. From one end to the other of New England came reporters hurrying to the village."

(*Page 124*)

In the sitting room of the Coolidge home they found the editor of the Ludlow paper, with a young soldier, the commander of the local Legion post and a reporter or two. Down the valley linemen were working stringing the first telephone wire into Plymouth. It came at two o'clock in the morning and a message from Washington brought to the Vice-President a strong suggestion from the Secretary of State to take the oath at once. In the two hours of waiting half a dozen Boston reporters had found their way to Plymouth. And there, surrounded by the newspaper men, and a few old friends, Calvin Coolidge, putting his hand on the family Bible, took the oath as President of the United States, administered by his father, the rural justice of the peace—a simple ceremony set in great dignity.

The reporters withdrew, the Coolidge house was darkened save for a light in the living room, and the Coolidges tried to sleep for a few hours until dawn. The President would not let the reporters photograph the inauguration. His taste always was good; his instincts decent and fine. After breakfast the reporters missed him. Then one of them saw him coming back from the little graveyard where his mother and sister lay. He had taken it all to them— the glory and the honor and the dread that must have gripped his heart. Slowly and abashed, staring at the ground, he passed the reporters and walked on into his new life.

Calvin Coolidge was the first President in seventy years to enter the White House from New England politics. His New England predecessor was Franklin Pierce, another conservative, also a patriot whose motives were pure, whose courage was unquestioned, and who, scorning the emotional appeal of high causes, did his cold logical best to save his country from disaster. Pierce also entered the practice of law in Northampton, Massachusetts, and mounted with much the same modesty as Coolidge the lower rungs of the political ladder. His police strike was a battle in Mexico. The New England sense of property in Pierce's heart gave him a distaste for disturbers of traffic, idealists, abolitionists, agitators, visionaries who would change the world. For the first time in nearly three-quarters of a century the American people again were in the mood which called Pierce from his New Hampshire fastness in 1852. In that much, at least, history was ready to repeat itself.

As Calvin Coolidge walked past the reporters from the graves of his ancestors into the greater cycle of his career that July day in 1923, no other American President ever carried more strongly on his face and in his mien the picture of a deep sense of heavy duty than he. The rugged tradition of five generations of Coolidges sleeping in the Vermont hills was upon him. A student's catalogued knowledge of what those traditions meant to the world was in his mind. And in his heart, all hidden

COOLIDGE FAMILY LOT IN PLYMOUTH CEMETERY

"Five generations of Coolidges sleep in the Vermont hills. . . He had taken it all to them—the glory, the honor, and the dread that must have gripped him."

(Page 125)

by reserves but there to guide him, was a passionate
fire of most orderly patriotic zeal which until that
hour had made his life a sacrifice to the deep yearning to serve his country in the one medium he understood—our American politics. To the outward view
that day in the tiny village among the green hills
of Vermont, Coolidge was a most unheroic figure—
walking with short, catlike steps, holding his eyes
upon the ground, with his slim body expressing the
merest commonplace, without the joy of youth nor
the challenge of strength. Yet within, the banked
fires must have glowed hot with the satisfaction of
a life's desire—the opportunity to serve—a desire
too deep and too sacred for pose, for grand gesture, for dramatic trick. Perhaps, trudging up the
hilly street of his native town, too dazed and awed
to strut, he had a cankering pride to appear in this
high moment just the commonplace Vermonter, in
his best black Sunday suit. For that was exactly
what he seemed!

CHAPTER XIII

THE RISE OF A NEW DYNASTY

The inauguration of Calvin Coolidge as President of the United States in the light of the coal-oil lamp in the Vermont farmhouse marked a new era in Republican politics.

A new dynasty appeared. For ten years a group of conservative leaders in the Republican organization, chiefly centering about the senatorial leaders, had dominated Republican politics and Republican conventions and Republican caucuses in Congress. These leaders were known as the Old Guard. Custom had staled them. They were becoming corrupt. In Ohio they were disreputable. In many states of the Middle West they shielded petty grafters and became patronage brokers of a rather mean sort. In many states of the South the old Republican organization was frankly mercenary. And everywhere, North, South, East and West, the Republican Party organization—the machine—was becoming merely an organized addiction for office; caring little about Republican principles, which as a matter of fact were not radically different from Democratic principles. In many states Republican leaders were the messenger boys of Big Business, puppets of a ruling local plutocracy, mannikins growing rather too powerful for the wires that joined them. They were becoming the masters and not the servants, were these political leaders, and revolt spread among the master classes, who are essentially honest according to their lights, despising graft and tolerating the grafters only when it is highly profitable or sadly necessary to do so.

Coolidge was not of the Old Guard. For nearly thirty years he had lived in politics, rising every biennium in power but never aligning himself with the crooked forces of his own party. He came from a liberal state where the Republican Party had become fairly conservative but never dirty. He came to Washington out of a civilization where every penny had pincher dents on it and where, in public expenditures, every dollar was accounted for. He came with no hangers-on, with no machine, with no friends to reward, no enemies to punish.

The Coolidges coming from Plymouth to the White House in midsummer of 1923, at first had rather a lonesome time. Somewhat their isolation was due to the fact that summer in Washington is hot, deserted, socially dead, and somewhat their position was due to the fact that they were truly strangers in the town. The politicians in charge of the Republican Party who had patronized Coolidge during the campaign of 1920, who had shunted him off to the South to make speeches where he could do no harm, who had acknowledged him as Vice-President only to make him the butt of their jokes, and who had regarded him as a New England freak, could not pull themselves together quickly enough to realize him as a President. During his two years as Vice-President, he had made little headway in political Washington, and outside of Washington in the country he had attracted no interest. His accession to power was followed by no enthusiasm. The summer waned and autumn came. Gradually Washington returned from its summer holiday and found the atmosphere of the White House changed entirely from that of the Harding régime. And the change was not due chiefly to the fact that the White House was going through a period of mourning for the dead President. The change in the White House was a change of dynasty. The social coterie that had surrounded President Harding found scant welcome with President Coolidge. The good-fellowship between the President and the Republican senators which Harding had maintained, Coolidge did nothing to encourage. He was polite; indeed courteous, punctiliously so, but he was not a back-slapper and hand-shaker. He had no stories to tell, no good fellows about him to cheer him up. The faithful Francis Stearns came down from Boston now and then to spend the week-end with the President; occasionally a Massachusetts friend dropped in but, speaking rather broadly, a new generation had arrived, a generation that "knew not Joseph." So the various Joes and Toms and Bills and Jims of Republican politics were gently, coolly, but rather inexorably, frozen into their proper places.

The new President's first public act upon coming to the White House was to join the Congregational Church. He has been a Congregationalist by birth, environment and attendance for many years. Mrs. Coolidge and his children were members of the church in Northampton. Even before he was sworn in as President, apparently something in his nature called out for a definite statement of his faith. It was characteristic of him that, in those days when his heart was troubled by the things of the spirit, he doggedly went to work inquiring, reading, fitting himself for an intelligent and final decision. That decision seemed to come to him in Plymouth before Harding's death. There was no Congregational church in Plymouth, so he took his time, as he always did. Then came Harding's death.

The spiritual impact upon any man who assumes the Presidency—the tremendous weight of responsibility, the astounding consciousness never leaving him, that something of the fate of 100,000,000 Americans, and through them all men in the civilized world, rests upon his decisions, upon his smallest daily acts—gives the man a new relation to life, shakes him fearfully in his innermost heart. When he arived at Washington from Plymouth to enter the White House for the first time as its master, the precise processes of his mind and heart had their

creed ready. Probably some of the New England
Congregational pastors with whom Coolidge had
been talking, to whom he had been writing for
books, let the Congregationalists in Washington
know something of the state of the President's feeling. Without notifying him of their action, the
officers of a local Congregational church elected him
to membership. The next Sunday he went to church
as a member, without spectacular initiation, in perfect Coolidgean fashion.

Yet in those months of peaceful administrative
delight, before Congress first met after the Coolidges came to the White House, the President knew
and the people realized that combat lay before him
with the opening of Congress. As a warrior he has
never made a fine figure. Always he has dramatized
himself indifferently; perhaps with dogged determination not to be a demagogue; perhaps because
he has no dramatic sense. In a fight he has generally
stood looking down his nose with a certain stubbornness in his countenance and an exasperatingly meek
determination in his mien and bearing. In those
months of congressional recess he went twice a week
to the newspaper conference, where bright young
reporters from every important city in America and
most of the capitals of the world assembled to question him.

Instead of appearing as the stern, strong, omniscient leader at these conferences, he slipped into the
meeting without a word, with scarcely a nod or a

greeting. He looked bored, with a certain touch of discouragement in his boredom. The ordeal was unpleasant. It is the time-honored custom of the conference that newspaper men shall write their questions and submit them to the President. This President read the first question in the budget, put it down, uttered no word, read the next, passed it, and when at last he came to a question which interested him, he read it aloud and answered it laconically rather than specifically, cautiously but not evasively, though weary withal. When he spoke definitely it was without much force; when he spoke indefinitely it was without any humor. Such was the attitude which he turned to the reporters when he was in his happiest days with Congress far away. Such was the attitude which the reporters in turn had reflected to their readers as "the White House attitude" upon any given public question.

Inevitably came a clash with Congress, which meant not primarily with the Democratic and Progressive leaders of Congress, but with the accredited Republican leaders as well. They thought they took his measure after his first message to Congress. He manifestly issued an invitation to Russia to open negotiations looking to recognition. Rumor in the Senate declared that this invitation came because Senator Borah desired it. But it was an obvious invitation. Russia responded. The American Secretary of State replied bitterly to the advances of Russia, discrediting the President; also angering

Borah.   Congress had no love for Borah and penniless Russia.   But it felt that the President could be ignored by Congress if he could be ignored by the Secretary of State.   The President had one major request to make of Congress: to follow the plan of the Secretary of the Treasury in the matter of reducing the surtaxes, which his enemies declared would reduce the taxes of the rich.   Congress blatantly ignored that request.   The President declared dogmatically against the bonus for veterans of the World War.   Congress passed the bonus bill.   He vetoed it.   Congress passed it over his veto.   And as the bill was going over the Presidential veto in the Senate, no one sat more complacently by, smiling like a cat with cream on its whiskers, than Senator Lodge, the Republican leader in the Senate, the senator from Coolidge's own state.   The President desired the Japanese Immigration restriction bill to be worded so that Japan would not be offended. His wishes were ignored and his veto overridden. The President felt that the pay of postal employees could not be increased until postal rates were increased.   Congress increased their pay.   The Republican leaders and the Republican whip in both houses could not be relied upon to support the President.   Congress was out of bounds.   It was the Old Guard, not the La Follette wing of the party, that was in rebellion against President Coolidge.   It was the crowd that named Harding which overcame the President in Congress before 1925.   And somewhat, though not entirely, it was the Republican Party of the West, the regular Republicans of the West, that allied themselves with the Democrats of the South, and the Progressives that President Coolidge could not control, much less lead.   During the first year and a half in the White House before his election in 1924 and the inauguration that followed it, President Coolidge was following the familiar curve of his life.   He was back in Amherst, a freshman again, back in the legislature a "singed cat," back in the state senate serving his first term, back in the governor's chair learning the game.   He seemed to learn it.   Never did a party leadership take more reluctantly a Presidential nominee than the Republican leaders took Coolidge in 1924.   They took him only because the rank and file of the party demanded it.

CHAPTER XIV

THE CORONATION AND THE REVOLT OF THE BARONS

The nomination of President Calvin Coolidge as a candidate for President was not a foregone conclusion when he entered the White House. Indeed, during the first few weeks or perhaps the first few months of his incumbency, certain conservative Republican leaders affected to assume that Coolidge would not aspire to the Presidential nomination. There was a general air of patronizing condescension toward the new President. Congress met in December, 1923, for its long session. The President's message at that session was not inspiring, yet it was dignified and explicit. But dignity and clarity are not qualities which in themselves produce leadership. The Senate of the United States during the Harding administration had been taking leadership away from the White House, more or less with the President's consent, if not with his actual connivance. The senatorial group which controlled the Republican National Convention of 1920 was in control of government. It could make no terms with the White House when Coolidge came there as President. That group frankly despised Coolidge and his kind. It was hard for that group to realize that it would have to take Coolidge as its Presidential candidate in 1924.

But gradually the realization came. The excuses which the senatorial group gave for accepting Coolidge's nomination were not reasons; the excuses were that to precipitate another candidacy would be to precipitate another fight in the convention; that no one else in sight could command a majority of the convention; that it might be a Democratic year anyway. The reason why the senatorial group ceased hoping to defeat Coolidge for the Republican Presidential nomination was the obvious fact that Coolidge was getting stronger and stronger with the American people. His character, his political methods, his point of view were fitting into a popular mood. So, rather grudgingly, the senatorial leaders of the Republican Party accepted Coolidge. They met without enthusiasm at the Republican Convention in Cleveland in June, 1924, to nominate President Coolidge and make him President in his own right by election.

A curious convention was that convention of 1924. The Old Guard was there but not in command. Command in the convention was assumed by William M. Butler, of Massachusetts, a textile manufacturer and friend of the President. He was a new man in national politics. He had served in Massachusetts as chairman of the state committee

of his party. He had been in the state senate with
Coolidge. He was a business man and he ran the
Cleveland convention as the head of an industrial
organization runs his plants. The Old Guard took
orders. Its members were messenger boys or sulked
and refused to do errands. Senator Lodge, who had
discredited the President in Congress, was himself
discredited, an outcast in the Republican Convention.
Ordinarily he would have been chairman of the
committee on resolutions or chairman pro tem of the
convention. Neither honor came to him, nor was he
consulted seriously about the policies of the new administration which were to be formulated in the
Republican platform. Senator Butler picked a candidate for Vice-President, Judge Kenyon, of Iowa,
failed to nominate him, and the convention, having
served its real master faithfully and well by nominating President Coolidge and adopting his platform,
followed the example of the convention four years
before and of many another convention. It broke
away from its nominal leadership and named its
own man for Vice-President, first former Governor
Lowden, who refused the nomination, and then Gen.
Charles G. Dawes. General Dawes would not have
been chosen as a Vice-Presidential candidate by the
Butler management of the convention. Neither was
he the choice of the senatorial crowd. He was a
child of chance; the result of revolt against orders,
a revolt which partly came from the Old Guard and
partly came from the delegates themselves. New

England was too obvious in the convention. The West and the South rebelled; hence Dawes.

In the campaign that followed, the stage management of the Presidential candidate was bad. He was smocked and put to pitching hay in Vermont. He was touted as the poor man's candidate. No more obvious, cynically conscious demagoguery ever was flaunted in the faces of the American people than the methods used in the campaign of 1924 to promote the candidacy of President Coolidge. He won, not because of this demagogy, but in spite of it. Through it and over it, he appealed to something in the American heart. He developed talent as a radio speaker. He spoke slowly, used short sentences, discarded unusual words, was direct, forthright and unsophisticated in his utterances. And so, over the radio, he went straight to the popular heart. His radio campaign helped greatly because it is one of the few campaign mediums by which the President always appears with his best foot forward. During the campaign he had little to say and said it well. In a year of confusion and babbling his reticence was unanswerable. Also the situation resolved itself into a contest not between Calvin Coolidge and John W. Davis, his Democratic opponent, but between Coolidge and either Bryan, the Democratic Vice-Presidential candidate, or possibly La Follette, who was out seeking the radical vote. Three parties in the field made it possible to throw the election into the House of

Representatives and finally into the Senate. And the threat of the election of the Democratic Vice-Presidential candidate by the Senate or the election of La Follette in the House added the excess to the Coolidge majority. He would have won at any rate, but the millions piled upon his majority by the fear of La Follette were unfortunate; for the millions of majority made his election rather meaningless, took away his personal triumph and somewhat made it an anti-La Follette or anti-Bryan victory. Coolidge deserved better of the country than that. Yet there were the votes. The vote-getter in Massachusetts became the vote-getter in America.

The knowledge that he is a born vote-getter, that he has popular claim, that the people are in his mood and trust him because he is what he is, always has given Coolidge a certain mild assurance. He has always had his proper pride. One day in the winter of 1925, after the election, twenty members of the House of Representatives filed into the White House to ask for a certain place for Governor Groesbeck, of Michigan, which the President might have bestowed. He sat facing the group, listened silently, with no indication in his countenance of his feeling about Governor Groesbeck. At last, when the delegation had talked itself down and had no other word to say, he spoke up rather coldly, something like this:

"Now, gentlemen, the resolution overriding my veto to the postal salaries bill is pending in the

House. I am interested in it. How many of you
are with me? I should like an expression."

The delegation was astounded. No such crass
interference by the White House with the power of
Congress ever had been seen before. The leaders of
the delegation had been fighting the President's
veto. But the other members of the delegation
spoke up in a friendly way. Finally the President
said:

"That will do, a pretty fair showing," and proceeded to clip out some dry noncommittal comment about the candidacy of Groesbeck. The delegation retired, and on the front steps of the White
House made loud lamentation. Nevertheless the
President's demonstration had its effect. The Senate voted to sustain the veto, but with nicely tem-
pered irony in the vote, sustaining it by one more
than the necessary one-third minority, leaving a
definite impression in the White House that the
Republican congressional leadership had studied that
sustaining vote rather too carefully. The situation
created an armed truce, which made it obvious that
all the stage-managing of the campaign and all the
tremendous Coolidge majority would not help the
President if he had attempted the strong kind of
leadership which Roosevelt or Wilson essayed. It
was very likely the battle of the two Coolidge myths
in the hearts of congressmen never entirely ended
even in the Republican caucus that produced a tension
in Washington while Congress recessed. Congress-

men and senators, after nearly three years' acquaintanceship, did not know the President. Less than any President in a generation did they understand this one. So congressmen and senators fell into two hostile camps; those who believed in the superman Coolidge and those who believed in the minus man Coolidge; adherents contending for the strong, wise, silent man and opponents hooting at the dull, lucky, dumb little man. Yet some way, out of all the doubt in high places, a real man has emerged in the lower levels. Instinctively the people estimate Coolidge for what he is. They understand his strength. They allow for his obvious limitations.

It is significant that during his four years in Washington and his thirty months in the White House, Coolidge made no open enemies—no one dared to defy him publicly. But, alas, neither did he make any strong friends in Congress, no affectionate and devoted followers to defend him against those who secretly plot against him! He seemed to be insulated against any emotional contact, whether of hatred or devotion.

After the election, at the short session of Congress, his New England friends presumed that leadership would be acknowledged to the President without question. But alas, electoral majorities never make leadership. Leadership does not come from afar. It springs out of the qualities in a man's own heart. Coolidge, as a legislative leader, as the titular head of his party, was no stronger after the tremendous majority of November, 1924, than he was before that majority was polled. Congress ignored him. The Republican organization in the Senate snubbed and the Democrats backed up the Progressives when they insulted him. Yet there was no revolt or protest from the people. Coolidge did not ask for the protest—did not arouse it. Revolt and protest come only when the spirits are summoned from the vasty deep, and Coolidge could not call them. He had never called them in his career. Probably he never will. It was not the radicals entirely, not the farm bloc, not even the La Follette following that snubbed and insulted the President during the short session of Congress from December, 1924, until March 4, 1925. It was somewhat Mid-Western Republicans of a rather strict party caste. During his eighteen months in office, Congress had done two most unusual things to the President. It had demanded the resignation of two Cabinet officers and refused to confirm the nomination of a third. No more illuminating example of a President's weakness as a legislative leader could have been developed. There was hatred for Wilson in the revolt of the Senate during the last two years of his term. There was fear of Roosevelt in the glee with which the regular party members of Congress bade his policies farewell after the election of 1908. But there was no emotion at all, either of hatred or fear, certainly not of active contempt even in the attitude of

Congress toward the President from the time he assumed office in July, 1923, until his inauguration in March, 1925. And the strange thing about the revolt of Congress in those twenty months was that the American people—indeed loyal and pharisaical Republicans—did not protest. Their votes indicated their respect for the President. But he could not rally them. Their support did not help him in his contests with Congress. The calm of his emotions begot calm in their hearts. Their respect which amounted to admiration for certain of his high qualities, never glowed into affection. The new dynasty had conquered the people; but they did not rise to put down the revolt of the barons.

Inauguration Day, March 4, 1925, was a fair day. "The Coolidge luck," said politicians. The President rode to his inauguration with Mrs. Coolidge and Senator Curtis, of Kansas, the official Republican Senate leader. Mrs. Coolidge smiled at every one. Curtis, proud of his position, put his gloves on in the carriage, a free, gay spirit from the wild and woolly West. He was obviously and conspicuously cheerful. But the President, going down to his inauguration, glowering at the end of his nose, made a doleful countenance in a felicitous hour. Possibly the trouble in his heart that reflected itself on his countenance was the congressional salary bill that awaited the President at the other end of Pennsylvania Avenue. The bill increased the salaries of the Senate and of the House of Representatives.

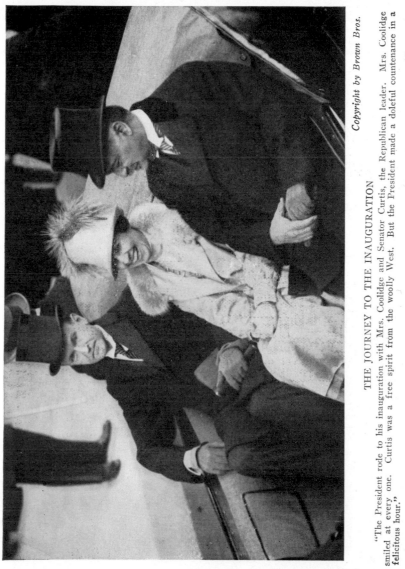

THE JOURNEY TO THE INAUGURATION

"The President rode to his inauguration with Mrs. Coolidge and Senator Curtis, the Republican leader. Mrs. Coolidge smiled at every one. Curtis was a free spirit from the woolly West. But the President made a doleful countenance in a felicitous hour."

(Page 144)

The bill was passed by Congress in the face of the President's demand for economy. The passage of the bill by Congress added the direct insult to a year and a half of thinly veiled neglect. For if the election of 1924 meant anything, it meant that the President's policy of economy was endorsed by the country. Yet here was an unmistakable denial of that policy. Moreover, the nomination of Charles B. Warren, the President's choice for Attorney General, was held up by the Senate. No one knew what the President would do with the congressional salaries increase bill; no one knew what he thought about the delay of the Senate in confirming Warren. But the President's countenance showed his perturbation of spirit. It clearly was ruining the day for him! It was his way. He could not have wreathed his angular countenance in a gay and felicitous smile without appearing as a conscious hypocrite impersonating a cheerful idiot. He could not pose. He would not pretend. He did not unbend to pay tribute to the hour and the multitude about him. One may regret his manners, but one cannot deny the force of his resolution, the dignity of his soul.

He came to the Capitol, went to the President's room in the Senate wing of the Capitol and sat him down to sign the waiting bills. He took up the bill providing for the congressional salary increases, the bill that he disliked. Maybe he had not decided what he would do with it. At least he sat for a long time glumly, looking at it, withholding his signature, saying no word but miserably troubled in mind. He looked at his hands and found thereon some speck of dust that distressed his orderly mind. Then suddenly he rose, walked briskly to a washroom, returned with damp, meticulous hands, took up the pen without a word, signed the obnoxious bill, rose, paced out of the room and went on to the end of his path of glory, his mind at ease, his face relaxed. That bill was a law; a part of the Established Order. His doubts were behind him. Returning from the inauguration some happy spirit captured him. He smiled, even waved his high hat once or twice in a genuine attempt at cordiality as Mrs. Coolidge laughed and smiled and poured through her gay countenance the pride and joy that was in her heart.

So the new dynasty—ruled by an honest, intelligently courageous, but soberly cautious conservative—came into power in the land!

AFTER HE WAS INAUGURATED

"After his inauguration some happy spirit captured him. He smiled, even waved his high hat once or twice in a genuine attempt at cordiality."

(*Page 146*)

CHAPTER XV

President Calvin Coolidge's first inaugural address was a short, businesslike document. In it the new President emphasized economy and tax reduction as a domestic problem and the entrance to the World Court as America's first duty abroad. This issue of economy is somewhat a matter to be settled by administration. Tax reduction is a legislative function. And of course our entrance into the World Court depends upon the United States Senate. But throughout the address it was the administrator unconsciously talking to the American people, not the legislative leader. Clearly, President Coolidge had no elaborate domestic legislative program. Obviously he was trying to let administration catch up with legislation.

Senator Charles Curtis, of Kansas, riding at the head of the inaugural procession down Pennsylvania Avenue with President Coolidge to the Capitol, March 4, 1925, rode as official Senate leader of the Republican Party, second in command in the United States government. The stark pine platforms along the path of glory had not been removed before trouble came to the White House—trouble that came, by the way, through the consolidation of the functions of government—and with trouble Curtis came as the President's first aid. It was one of those quick transformations, that coming of trouble, which changes triumph to tragedy. The President, before his inauguration, had made it plain that he desired Charles B. Warren, of Michigan, to be Attorney General of the United States. If the Senate had not been given veto power over executive appointments, the President should have had the right to name his legal adviser. It was obvious even before the formal announcement of Mr. Warren's appointment, that he was objectionable to a considerable minority at least of the United States Senate. He had incurred the enmity of Senator Couzens, a Republican progressive, of Michigan, who made personal cause against Warren in the Senate. That in itself might have defeated him, but more important than the protest of Senator Couzens was the opposition of Senator Borah, of Idaho, and the group that followed him. Their opposition was based upon the connection of Mr. Warren as attorney with the so-called sugar trust. The trust had been investigated by the Senate; Warren, its attorney, in representing the trust had been unable successfully to defend his methods before the Senate committee. They were regarded by many senators as iniquitous; and immoral if not illegal. Naturally, the Democratic minority, always glad to make trouble for the Republican Party, furnished what may be termed votes of convenience to Borah and Couzens. The La Follette group, of course, denounced the Warren appointment. Senator Curtis, officially as Republican Senate leader, had warned the President that the confirmation of Mr. Warren as Attorney General by the Senate was in extreme doubt.

Then there was another angle of danger; the new Vice-President, Mr. Charles G. Dawes, being freshly inaugurated, had harangued the Senate upon its lax methods and, what he deemed to be, its archaic rules. The President by no means sponsored the Dawes attack, but was held by many members of the Senate and by the people at large responsible for it. At least, the President did not formally and specifically rid himself of the odium in the Senate and elsewhere which followed the Dawes pronunciamento against the Senate. The Senate, therefore, was generally in a low frame of mind about the White House. The Senate was in special session to consider, among other things, the confirmation of Mr. Warren. It was known that a tie vote existed. The President and Senator Curtis, the leader of the Senate, had reason to expect that the Vice-President would be in the Senate chamber to cast the deciding vote for Mr. Warren, and so break the tie. Suddenly the Democrats forced a vote upon the Warren confirmation. The Vice-President was absent. He was asleep at his room in the hotel. Senator Curtis sent for him. A taxicab came flying from Dawes's hotel to the Capitol, as the vote proceeded. The taxicab was too slow. Dawes was late. The Vice-President did not arrive in time and Warren failed to be confirmed. The President was discredited. The seven million majority at the polls was ignored and the legislative leadership of Calvin Coolidge suffered the loss of prestige which comes with defeat.

In the meantime, while the Warren candidacy was being considered by the Senate, Mr. Warren was a guest at the White House. After the debate, Senator Curtis hurried to the White House to tell the President that it would be unwise to submit Warren's name again. But against the advice of Curtis, who certainly knew the Senate better than any one else, and possibly out of deference to his house guest, the President refused to abandon Warren. Now, President Coolidge's attitude toward Warren is typical. Warren, as an agent of the sugar interests, was the attorney of a majority unit of investors of capital, representing many millions of dollars. That capital was and is property. In manipulating the affairs of the sugar trust, certainly Mr. Warren was protecting that property, and promoting those interests. That incidentally he was not protecting the common interests of the people of the United States was a matter of secondary consideration to a man of the President's point of view. He has declared often and definitely that if property is conserved, civilization is advanced; the manner and morals of the men who at the moment happen to be conserving the property do not seem to interest the President as much as the faithfulness and the efficiency of these men in protecting the property in question for its honest owners. Warren was good enough to represent the White House in Mexico, he was good enough to be chairman of the committee that drafted the platform for the Republican National Convention. A man who had occupied those two places had, according to the rules of the game, as the President knows the game, washed himself clean of any obloquy which the Senate investigation may have put upon him. But in the debate upon the question of Warren, and in the newspaper uproar which followed the debate, all that Warren had done for the sugar trust became fresh fodder for the hungry and clamoring mob of Democrats, Progressives and finical citizens with moral scruples about the importance of the public welfare in the organization of trusts.

Again, after the President's public insistence upon the confirmation of Warren, in spite of one defeat, Curtis called at the White House and again told the President that defeat was inevitable, that votes had changed which once had stood with Warren; that the lost prestige of defeat had broken the President's power in the Senate. The President was then willing to listen to Senator Curtis. The President told Curtis to return to the Senate and, to use a political phrase, to "feel out" the sentiment of the Senate toward the President's old friend from Ludlow, Vermont, John Garibaldi Sargent. Sargent was a wooldyed conservative who had represented certain property interests before the Vermont legislature; a man of high standing as a lawyer, of unimpeachable character, and decent legal associations. Curtis returned to the Senate, and canvassed the senators to see if Mr. Sargent could be confirmed. Naturally, the senators who were approached about the Sargent candidacy hurried to tell their reporter friends of the President's changed attitude. Remember that Mr. Warren was still in the White House. The reporters, hearing that the President was considering another candidate for Attorney General, hurried to tell their editors. The editor of the Washington *Evening Star* hurried to tell his readers in an early edition which reached the White House just before noon, just before the President was going to lunch with his guest, Mr. Warren. There it was; the news in glaring headlines, that the President had abandoned his house guest and was considering his older friend from Ludlow, Vermont, for the place as Attorney General. An embarrassing quarter of an hour ensued. It was given out rather testily from the White House and with some spirit that the President had no idea of abandoning Mr. Warren's candidacy, and that if the Senate rejected it again the President would name Mr. Warren as a recess appointment. That was a sad, mad mistake, and extremely bad strategy. It in effect denied to the

Senate its constitutional right to advise and consent to the President's appointments. For thirty-six hours all the busy bees of the Senate swarmed at the name of Coolidge, and stung it. There was riot in the headlines of newspapers. The President had challenged the Senate. He must either fight or back down. Again Curtis came to the White House, advising the President to conciliate the Senate. Mr. Warren, in a spasm of good taste, left the White House, and the President, having no stomach for combat, retreated, cooled off, regained his poise, suppressed his emotions, and sent the name of Mr. Sargent, of Ludlow, Vermont, to the Senate for consideration as the Attorney General. Sargent was quickly confirmed. It was a revealing episode. The country knew then that the President had a short and crusty temper, a human attribute not to his discredit, and that he took counsel, finally, of his wiser hours rather than of his moments of vexation. No gargantuan wrath was revealed, no Jovelike anger. The President was vexed, that was all.

Cooling off, he had no face to save. He became the imperturbable Yankee gentleman who had never sacrificed the main chance to his vanity. Whatever the country may have learned of its President by the Warren incident the President surely learned to rely upon the wisdom, tact and loyalty of Charles Curtis, of Kansas, the second in command.

The American Constitution does not provide for a legislative leader in the White House. But when the

Constitution provided that administrative officers, including the members of the President's Cabinet, should be appointed with the consent of the Senate, it followed naturally that the members of the House of Representatives also would desire some control of patronage, and there Congress took upon itself administrative functions. Naturally any President having administrative relations with any Congress took on congressional leadership and came to have through the party system the actual functions of legislative leadership. A President has a legislative program. He has stood for legislative policies in the campaign. He has a duty to make his campaign pledges good, and so by swap, barter, coercion and persuasion, the President has become a part of Congress.

In the memory of men living in the first quarter of the twentieth century, every President of the United States has been a legislative leader—more or less. Since the Civil War, Hayes, Arthur and Harrison have exhibited distinct impulses to return to the Presidency of the Constitution; to become administrators rather than legislative functionaries with extra constitutional powers. But the pressure of the party system has been too much for them. Even Grover Cleveland, strong as he was, could not resist legislative leadership, and in the last quarter of a century the White House has become more and more a citadel of all the powers of government. Even the federal judiciary was recast to the liberal viewpoint by Roosevelt and Wilson and again turned back to the conservative viewpoint by Harding and Coolidge. The three nominal branches of government, the administrative, the legislative and the judicial, which were so nicely arranged to give America a system of checks and balances in government, are in fact, and what is more in the hearts of the people, held to be all of one branch—the government at Washington, incarnate in the man in the White House.

President Calvin Coolidge always has excelled as an administrator. His vanity has been fairly well concealed. But sometimes it has appeared in a stubborn refusal to do a thing which he knows he does poorly. Hence, perhaps unconsciously but definitely, President Coolidge, at the opening of the first elective term, was trying to emphasize the administrative part of his office. The legislative functions imposed by the party system probably irked him. He handled the courts instinctively, making them over into "vessels of wrath fitted unto destruction," the revolutionary agents of reactionary government, without realizing the implications of his handiwork. But when he put his hand to the plow at the Capitol at the other end of Pennsylvania Avenue, it was with a weary sense of distaste and futility. Perhaps this distaste and futility is the origin of the bad smell which seemed to be hanging around the end of his nose, as he drooped his tired eyes while he rode to his inauguration!

The President, during the first two years of his administration, devoted much of his executive energy to the enforcement of the prohibitory law. It was evident that be believed it should have a fair trial at strict enforcement. But also it was evident that he did not propose to evangelize and make sentiment for the Volstead Act—which was the one thing it needed. A word of exhortation to the ruling classes to take liquor from their homes out of respect to the law which had, by making liquor expensive, taken it largely from the homes of the poor—one such blast from the White House would have been worth a million dollars in administrative endeavor. But Coolidge could not say the word. Always he has been tongue-tied when he needed to make public sentiment by his words. He generally has spoken through his deeds. Sometimes they were not articulate; did not reach the popular ear.

The Senate in refusing the confirmation of Warren probably reflected the attitude of Congress toward President Coolidge. He was not master of the legislative situation, as Wilson was, or Roosevelt, or even at times Grover Cleveland. Congress seemed to be as determined that Coolidge should be a constitutional President as Mr. Coolidge himself was. His inaugural address had announced no legislative program, beyond economy, tax reduction and participation in the World Court. He had staked off no fighting ground. Legislation evidently meant little in his idea of a successful administration. The

spring became summer and the summer autumn
and still no legislative program came from the White
House. The President made few public addresses,
and said practically nothing of public interest. He
was devoting himself sedulously to administration.
Two years in the White House had taught him the
ropes. He enjoyed his work, freed from the pest of
Congress. He went into the reorganization of federal departments. He took a superintendent's joy
in coördinating and consolidating bureaus. Not in
years had the government had as its head a man who
was so devoted to the problems of administration.
Thus, until Congress met again with its insistent
problems, Calvin Coolidge tinkered happily at the
executive's job.

He had his diversions and enjoyed them. Parties
of a mild "church sociable" character gave him
some pleasurable reaction; quiet but real. Often
one saw him in the White House, not in the office-
building annex, but in the family rooms, a shy figure,
sometimes walking two or three times across one
end of a room and in and out of it, before being
able to turn to a friendly group chatting in the
corner. But when he turned, he appeared before
the group sometimes, if the members of the group
were strangers, standing a bit detached, throwing in
some detached little cosmic scrap of conversation,
unable to plunge into the midst of the social chatter.
Mrs. Coolidge and his son have stood in no great
awe of him. He has never been a stern, awesome

father in the Coolidge household. Openly and merrily they mock his quacking Vermont drawl, which mocking is the highest testimonial to the beautiful family relations that prevail in the White House.

The Coolidge bashfulness has not kept him a hermit. His taste for formal society was not for the kind of parties that Harding gave—select, jammed with stuffed lions, and sometimes too noisy with good fellows. The Coolidge parties, on the *Mayflower*, for instance, always have been made up by the President himself. It has been his habit to pick friends, or those whom he might come to know as friends. Then he avoided them and enjoyed them to the limit. It was his way—somewhat Vermont, somewhat peculiarly Coolidge of Vermont. He always has known that he was an odd one. When the moving-picture man attached to the White House was insisting that the party before the camera talk, to give animation to the picture, the President twanged appreciatively:

"That man gets more conversation out of me than all Congress!"

A most human man he is, back of the mask. When sorrow came to the Coolidges and their son, Calvin, died, the President was terribly broken. The boy was like his people, looked like his father, was a thoroughgoing Coolidge. Yet the President found few words to assuage his grief by releasing his expression of it. He was inarticulate in his woe. He did not let the storm of his heart reflect itself upon his face. He went through the whole heartbreaking public funeral ceremony, realizing that his office gave him no privacy. No flinch nor flicker on his face betrayed what his heart was enduring. A friend came to him in sympathy, spoke some gentle word, and after a silence the President said, as unemotionally as though he were discussing some remote and impersonal thing:

"Yes, he got a blister on his heel. Used iodine. Nothing could be done."

Just that. He looked mutely at the ground; the little boy in Vermont, again standing before the closed door—the door to the great mystery. Yet behind his motionless mask raged the tumult of his grief.

PART IV

THE HUMAN PROBLEM AT
WASHINGTON

CHAPTER XVI

A MAN EMERGES FROM THE MYTHS

The fact that Coolidge's birthday was on the Fourth of July is disturbing. Naturally the people expect a prodigy. And then, coming into life on the Fourth of July, he keeps climbing upward steadily in patriotic service, never abandoning his climb to cuddle down in an office of profit; nor resting to lay by an honest dollar, acting all the time like a person out of a school reader. These things breed hero tales. In a life wherein virtue is always being rewarded, wherein copy-book lines are forever coming true—and throughout the life of Calvin Coolidge the cross-stitch wall mottoes and samplers which encouraged three hundred years of New England piety and probity have been crashing out of their frames into gray pin-striped trousers and a frock coat—the all-too-superstitious masses are not to be blamed if they see signs and portents arising from simple things. Take the fact that this wordless man marries a girl from the deaf and dumb school. In a hapless world such Heaven-born order seems miraculous. And if one holds that perfect accord and complementary union are miraculous, then here is a miracle. For the marriage of Calvin Coolidge and Grace Goodhue is one of those Heaven-sent events designed to renew the flagging faith of humanity. Of course no one ever got eulogy of Mrs. Coolidge from her husband. Searching through interviews with him and books about him, one finds only half a dozen words of acknowledgment of this gift of God:

"She is a great help to me!"—no more!

But if he could have said more, such a woman would have been superfluous. As it is, she is a vital part of his success, of his life, of his happiness.

So let us consider Grace Anna Goodhue Coolidge, born a Vermonter, graduated from the state university, coming to the White House in her middle forties, handsome, animated, lovely of mien and manner, a brunette for her husband's blond, charming where he is silent, quick where he is slow, intuitive where he is logical. The whole union seems cabalistic, in some way occult, done by fairies or super-creatures—indeed, the Heaven-made marriage. One would say that, along with all the perfections which Calvin Coolidge has achieved, this marriage, in the one human area where the average of mischance is highest, just could not have happened. It is like that Fourth of July nativity for a man who walks straight through ten thousand absolutely insuperable objects straight to the White House. It just cannot be. But here it is, this marriage which completes a man and a woman by

MRS. CALVIN COOLIDGE

"It was Calvin Coolidge who taught her to round the heel in knitting a sock."

(Page 165)

spiritual synthesis. Mrs. Coolidge stands slightly
above the medium height for women, with a slender
figure and supple; a good dancer, a fine, firm
carriage, and a head poised for frankness. Candor
is the first characteristic of her face. Her eyes—
the come-hither kind—are larger than common.
Her brow is broad. Her nose is marked for strength
as well as beauty, but the strength of her face is in
her mouth, wherein is least beauty but most character. Clearly she is emotional. But obviously she
has herself in hand. It was she in the little room
at Plymouth whose eyes were wet when the reporters saw the Coolidges the hour when the news
of Harding's death came to them. But it was she
also, when her husband wrote his first statement
after his inauguration, who gathered the scattered
manuscript, sorted out the pages, and handed the
duplicate sheets to the reporters. She never leaves
her job. But no model of the household virtues
was Grace Goodhue. It was Calvin Coolidge who
taught her to round the heel in knitting a sock! He
learned how in Plymouth. Burlington, where Grace
Goodhue grew up, is a larger town than Plymouth.
She was a sophisticate who never learned knitting.

But she nevertheless conformed. In twenty
years, during which she has lived with a man with
a queer passion for public service, she has foregone
all that he has foregone, has sacrificed all that he
has, and more, considering the ways of women; has
played life's rather hard game, as the home-making

wife of an abnegating political ascetic who never made a dollar out of office. And through it all she has turned a laughing, defiant face at the fate that set her a bit apart from other women of her caste and kind. If any woman, seeing the end of the road, smiles, thinking it an easy way, let her live fifteen years, bringing up two children, and keep house without a maid, for a rising statesman! And if any woman envies the mistress of the White House, let that woman go down into the shadow of death and part with her son, and come back to a place where she cannot be sad, cannot show her grief, where duty demands that she cover her sorrow and turn a gay face to a forgetting world.

Like a wineglass elm in a Vermont meadow—alone, thin, slight, graceful but sturdy for all native winds and weathers, shedding a shy, indefinable sense of beauty rather in memory than in the eye—is this union of two lives that we know as Coolidge in the White House to-day. Yet, make no mistake, he is no shrine piece, this Coolidge, but a faulty man, who makes his mistakes like the rest of us. He keeps his word rather more inviolate than most politicians. But he is chary of it, and probably is not above giving a reason to one man for refusing to assume an obligation and an excuse to another; the reason and the excuse being quite different statements of fact about a situation in politics. No blurter or bawler-out of sheer raw truth is he. Yet intrigue irks him. He does not meet it with gusto as Roosevelt met it.

But he does not meet anything in life as Roosevelt met it. Neither does he let life overcome him as it defeated Harding, nor does he shrink from hard knocks as Wilson sometimes shrank. He stands often before questions, not answering them. But no cowardice silences him. His silence comes because he is not sure of the truth. A vain man would bluff. A daring man would chance it. A dishonest man would parley. Each of them probably would be happier before a problem than this silent, joyless, cautious man. Measure life any way one will, in terms of success or of satisfaction or of ease, almost any kind of man gets more fun out of existence than he of the cautious type. Probably Coolidge figures that his career has justified his theory of life; that pride in his Presidential office has made up for the joy he may have lost in getting there. There are those who would differ from him. Indeed, there are those who order their lives on a quite different theory, and end warming the stove in the village store. It's a matter of taste and choice.

His presence in the Cabinet meetings of President Harding, a voiceless, cool puritanical sphinx listening to the routine of business rolling across the Cabinet table, gave him a peculiar fitness to succeed Harding. Probably the Vice-President knew better than the President himself much of the general details of the Presidential office. Harding was inclined to be lazy, to leave his desk uncleared in the afternoon, to procrastinate, to avoid decisions, to let time change events and so soften the harsh edge of problems.

When President Coolidge came to the White House he brought a trained mind there. In passing, it may be noted that for the first time in American history both the President and his wife hold college degrees. The habit of application which the New England mind acquires easily, his four years at Amherst had settled into the rut of his life. To say that he has a clean and healthy brain, does not mean that he has a powerful mind, but it means that he has a physical organ in his cranium which will bear the strain of physical work, long and close application; a mind which, in the Coolidge case, works normally and logically, and in the end produces those normal and logical conclusions known as common sense. Whatever genius President Coolidge has developed has been the result of his capacity for hard work. He takes no short cuts, follows no hunches, sees few visions.

His slow processes of thought enforce the silent habit which is his outer characteristic. But they do more; they keep him humble and give him always an outer air of modesty which his inner opinion of himself may sadly belie. Certainly he has reason to be proud of himself. With his five talents, he has done more than most men with their ten. But because he plods slowly from syllogism to conclusion, where he sees others brilliantly sweeping by him upon intuitive processes to the truth, he has kept a humble if not a contrite heart. This humility marks every line of his contour, keeps him off his heels when he walks, and gives him almost but not quite a mincing gait. This consciousness of a slow process of reasoning downcasts his eye, and we see him forever staring down his nose.

As President of the United States Coolidge fitted into the national psychology, indeed, into the world psychology of these post-war days. The world as well as America is disappointed. It has had to give up so many of its ideals, to discard so many of its finalities, to stop, look and listen at every crossroad in its problem, fearing chaos. A cautious world turned logically—may we say mythologically? —to Cautious Cal. In turning it made a myth of him, indeed it made the two myths that have always surrounded him; the myth of the strong, dumb, omniscient creature who hurls thunderbolts out of silence, or—if you disagree with him—the meek, dull, lucky little man who sits tight and grabs quickly.

But underneath the myth the sense of reality came to the American people. The Coolidge that is, the Coolidge quite apart from the god-myth of his worshipers and the devil-myth of his enemies, projected his real qualities into the American heart. In 1910 the American people would not have accepted him. They were in no mood for him or his kind; they were adventurous. They admired daring. They were all for setting out upon grand pilgrimages to high goals. They followed Roosevelt and Wilson, men of aspiration, leaders who looked forward into a better day and a nobler time. But this third decade of our century is a decade of reaction from war. The people are not interested in large altruistic enterprises. They desire substantial things, and for themselves chiefly. They are trusting to the devil to care for the hindermost. In this mood they turned overwhelmingly to Coolidge. "Economy will solve the problems of our country," declared Coolidge, and the majority applauded. It really believed that. It refused to recognize problems which economy could not solve. So to all intents and purposes the ignored problems are just uncomfortable and unaccountable facts. The men and women who followed Roosevelt to Armageddon, and those who aspired with Wilson to a peaceful world, seem to be submerged; and the great majority which these leaders once commanded has disintegrated.

Coolidge symbolizes rather than leads conservatism. He lacks the daring of leadership. His courage is of another quality, which makes neither converts nor crusaders, but which does hold the fort.

This may be his epitaph: "As a leader of conservatism, he rallied few converts; but he made no mistakes."

CHAPTER XVII

THE SENATE LEADER AND THE PRESIDENT

Since Woodrow Wilson lost his leadership of the world and his own country in 1919, America has been led, if not governed, by the United States Senate. President Wilson, broken in health, struggled tragically to hold his leadership. Presidents Harding and Coolidge strove as impotently, if not so tragically, to keep the hollow forms of leadership in the White House. Harding struggled perhaps only to save his face; Coolidge to save the Constitution. President Harding came from the Senate, nominated by a senatorial cabal controlling the Republican National Convention of 1920. Partly by way of courtesy but sometimes after a mild contest, the Senate let Harding save his Presidential face. In return for the senatorial kindness, President Harding allowed the Senate to entrench itself in power. The powerful senatorial blocs which formed under Harding continued to function under President Coolidge——the agrarian bloc, and the so-called irreconcilables; one bipartisan, the other for the most part Republican. When President Coolidge came to the White House the Senate broke the entente. By resolution the Senate demanded changes in the President's Cabinet. Two members, Denby and Daugherty, left under senatorial pressure. The Senate then refused to confirm the appointment of Charles B. Warren, whom President Coolidge named as a member of his Cabinet. The blocs were unchecked. Vice-President Dawes, coming in with the new Coolidge administration in March, 1925, railed against blocs; complained at the minority control of the Senate, which was in reality the soul of the senatorial cabal, and by reason of the Vice-Presidential clamor the people came to realize the situation, which is in effect a revolutionary change in our government. For if the Senate wins its fight for leadership in American government the Presidential office must decline in prestige and power until it logically will become little better than the presidency in France and in Germany—a figurehead in government.

Entering his first elective term, President Coolidge found the Senate organized, not against him, but quite independently of him. His pious determination to be merely a constitutional President, so far as congressional leadership went, made his tremendous popular majority a cinema victory. During the first part of Coolidge's first elective term, the Senate led Congress in ignoring the President's leadership and so the Senate initiative in government ruled the land.

Now the Senate leadership is nominally and ac-

tually in the hands of Charles Curtis, of Kansas, a
senator of the United States since 1907, barring
a lapse of two years when he fell among the Rooseveltian Philistines. He came to Congress in 1893,
and spent fourteen years in the House of Representatives before coming to the Senate. He was
elected to his first office, county attorney of Shawnee County, Kansas, in 1884, and barring six years
of "rest from his loved employ" has been in office
for forty years. The historian studying those
times must take account of Curtis of Kansas under
Coolidge quite as much as historians must know
about Gorman in Grover Cleveland's day, or of
Don Cameron in Lincoln's day or of John Hancock
in Washington's day. The historian studying our
times, going over the history of legislation for
thirty years, will not find Curtis's name attached
to any measure of first importance. Upon the
floors of Congress he has contributed nothing to
the economic thought, to the great national tendencies. He has had few pet measures and the few
were unimportant. Yet several times, standing
upon the floor of the Senate, he has spoken briefly
in commonplace sentences, introducing motions of
procedure, or even motions to adjourn, but thereby
has vastly controlled national destinies. For he is
the voice of the organization. To him top hats
sway; from his hand statesmen eat or starve. He
is a good and perfect gift of American politics—a
first ranker in politics, who knows no other calling,

who has survived for forty years in it, and has remained a poor man, against whom no suspicion ever has pointed; whose name always has been clean.

Curtis, considered as a product of blood and habitat, is easily explained as a leader. In his veins are three potent strains of inheritance—Indian, French and New England. In the early part of the nineteenth century, Curtis's great-grandfather, a Frenchman living near St. Louis, married the daughter of White Plume, a Kaw Indian chief. She was the granddaughter of Chief Pawhuskie, of the Osage tribe. Julie Conville, the daughter of this Indian woman, married Louis Pappan, a French trader near St. Louis in the middle of the nineteenth century and the Pappans moved with the Kaw Indians to their reservation in Kansas. Senator Curtis's grandmother, Julie Conville Pappan, had an Indian allotment—a farm near North Topeka, Kan., where Charles Curtis, the Senate leader, was born, the child of Ellen Pappan and Captain O. A. Curtis. Now the Curtises were from Indiana out of New England—old New England. His grandmother, Permilia Hubbard, came with her New England conscience from New Hampshire and her people, the Hubbards, came from Massachusetts, where they appeared in 1621. So back in the seventeenth century the Hubbards and the Coolidges were Massachusetts neighbors. Ten years later, in 1631, the Curtises landed in New

York. With the adventurers of freedom who rushed into Kansas in the mid-fifties came O. A. Curtis, in '56, who married the Indian girl and went to the Civil War and returned a brave soldier and a captain after the war of the sixties was over.

No mere political happen-so is Senator Charles Curtis. He is a product of blood as Coolidge is of environment. The scion of two Indian chieftains of more than local fame probably was going to be a leader of his fellows. The grandson of a Frenchman was going to have a certain charm and romantic flare in his life, while that Hubbard blood doomed him inexorably to a life-term servitude to details, dry, hard details that under his imagination were bound to take some definite shape in a constructive form.

The French and Indians got him first. His early career was romantic—as romantic as Coolidge's was drab. His mother died when he was three years old and the Curtis child went to the Kaw reservation, sixty miles west of Topeka, with his grandmother, Julie Pappan, who was living with her mother's people—reservation Indians. The illimitable prairie was there; hunting was a part of the child's daily life. Dogs and horses were the companions of babyhood and boyhood and at eight years old Charles Curtis was a jockey, riding races at the fairs. At ten he had a name in the state and at twelve he was a figure in his part of the world, a lithe, handsome, black-haired, black-eyed

boy, the Indian jockey—"ol' Cap Curtis's boy."
Contrast this figure with that of the little shy ten-
year-old in home-made clothes standing by the stone
schoolhouse in Plymouth. What poles they seem
apart!

Charles Curtis went back to his father's people
after the Cheyenne Indian raid in 1868 and lived
with his father's parents—the Curtises of New York
and New England. When the government sent the
Kaw Indians from Morris County, Kansas, to the
Indian Territory—where now Oklahoma is, the
little Curtis boy desired to go with his Grandmother
Pappan. He joined the tribal hegira. But the first
trek out of Topeka, his Grandmother Julie Pappan
came to him late at night and urged him to go back.
She told him what was ahead of him as a reservation
Indian; what might be his fortune if he lived with
the whites. It was the Pappans talking with the wisdom of their white French blood. The boy turned
back at dawn and walked to Topeka. In the winter
he went to school, in the summer and fall he followed the races. When he was sixteen years old he
had a winter contract for riding—a good one, worth
more money to him than his father could have made.
But again, a wise woman's voice spoke to him—
his grandmother, Permilia Hubbard Curtis, of New
Hampshire, persuaded him to quit the track and go
to school. So he went through the grades of the
common school and began life on his own. He
developed early. And, while he quit the races, he

still loved horses and, as a youth, drove the hotel bus that "made the trains" in Topeka. The New England blood called him, even in the livery stable. So the boy kept on reading books. He got a job as a reporter on a North Topeka paper, and in his late teens went about gathering news and soliciting subscribers.

Thus he began his political career. For he could remember names and faces, and all over Shawnee County he knew the names of men and women who were to be his first assets in politics. And here is where he got his first windfall—the inheritance from the Convilles and Pappans, his blessed gifts as a hand-shaker, a palaverer, the indefinable thing called charm which binds men to one forever. As he rose in Kansas politics, his more favored enemies upon whom he bestowed from time to time the bitter benediction of defeat, referred to him as "the Injun," or, being sarcastic, "the Noble Red Man of the Forest," or, for short, "Lo!" Be that as it may. He never has lost a friend or trusted an enemy in all his long and rising career.

How curiously different are the lines of these two lives, that of Curtis, the Plainsman, and Coolidge, the Green Mountaineer; lives that were to come together so closely in the third decade of the new century and to carry with them such power for good or evil in the history of mankind! Curtis, the little Indian jockey with his fantastic jockey clothes, was riding races the year Coolidge was born, driving a

bus, studying between hours in the livery stable as
Coolidge was coddled, a sheltered, shy and rather
lonely child, in his mountain home.

So with his French and Indian inheritance, Curtis
entered life. At nineteen he began studying law in
Topeka, and when he was twenty-one, he was
admitted to the bar and went straight into politics.
He was of course an organization man, and a
Republican by inheritance. He appeared at the city
and county conventions, in those first days of the
eighties in Topeka, with the names of hundreds of
farmers at his tongue's tip. He was a handsome
youth—slight, with the jockey's litheness, with affectionate, black, caressing eyes that were hard to forget; with a fine, olive skin, and a haymow of black
hair and a curling black mustache. Add to that a
gentle, ingratiating voice, and an easy flow of innocu-
ous conversation unimpeded by pestiferous ideas,
and you have a creature God-sent into politics. The
North Topeka folks called him "Our Charley." So,
when he was twenty-four years old, he was elected
prosecuting attorney of Shawnee County—the
county which contained the capital of the state of
Kansas. In 1880, four years before young Curtis
was made prosecuting attorney, Kansas had adopted
prohibition. The young man, whose fame as a
jockey was still fresh in the minds of his fellow citizens, was elected by the wets. They did not question him. They took it for granted that he was
with them. And then the day after his elevation

to office he went to work on the open saloons of
Topeka with all the energy of a crusader. The wets
had forgotten about Permilia Hubbard and the New
England conscience!

Curtis closed the saloons of Topeka. He was
triumphantly reëlected. At twenty-eight he retired
from office and became a criminal lawyer with an
assured practice. He made money; his law office
was busy. Every fall he went out campaigning for
the Republicans. But he spent his energy wisely.
He spoke generally in the Fourth Congressional
District—his home bailiwick, which then covered a
geographical area larger than a New England state.
It was in the spring of 1892, when Calvin Coolidge
was a scrawny freshman stepping on his feet at
Amherst, that they nominated "Our Charley" for
Congress at the Fourth District Convention in the
little town opera house at Emporia. Among the responsible politicians of the time and place, "Our
Charley" was not exactly as popular as the name his
friends gave to him indicated. But the politicians let
him go out against a milkman whom the Populists
nominated with the sweetly solemn thought that the
milkman would defeat him. But "Our Charley"
demolished the milkman, and that in a Democratic
year. He won by his personal charm—the palaver
of him. His enemies made the mistake of stressing
his Indian blood in ignominy. When he appeared
in a little town, and all the towns of the district
were little towns except Topeka, people turned out

to see the Indian. What they saw was a gallant
young Frenchman, suave, facile, smiling, with win-
ning ways and a handshake that was a love affair
in itself. The little, fat, bald-headed milkman with
a stubby chin whisker and a Holy Cause had no
show even in a Democratic year against "Our
Charley."

It was that year that Curtis began putting his
brains into politics. In every county of his district
he listed the names of those who had helped him—
and also those who had opposed him. He mem-
orized the names—no mean task. Only a man who
had a hard, sound brain could do it. He put the
names down geographically. He had a slip for each
township. He carefully and painstakingly asso-
ciated the names with the faces which belonged to
them. Whenever he had a letter from a citizen, he
answered it personally, recalling some incident of
their meeting. Whenever he was called into the
town or township, he read over his list, conjured up
the faces and called every one by his right name,
and asked some personal question of the man when
he met him or of him, if the man was absent, which
bound that man to the congressman for life. "Our
Charley," having weathered three elections, by 1896
was a figure in Kansas politics, by reason of his
brains. For it takes just as much brains, and brains
of just as high an order, to remember ten thousand
names and faces in a district, with something about
each name and face to distinguish it from all the

others, as it does to remember tariff schedules or the relation between the price of wheat and pig iron or bar silver in a given month for a half century.

It is interesting to note how these two men, Curtis and Coolidge, were storing their minds with exactly the kind of facts that would be needed for their coöperation thirty years ahead. Coolidge was studying history, economics, sociology, philosophy—things required if one has a broad grasp of the meaning of life. Curtis was studying men in those days. He was learning how affectionate they are and how prone to disloyalty; learning how wise they are and how foolishly they sometimes act, how self-interest reveals itself, and how far it pulls a man, and where it slips the belt for something deep and fine outside himself that makes a man a decent citizen. In the mud and moil of practical politics, "Our Charley" was getting that "O. C." degree, the only one he ever had, and in the shades of Amherst, Coolidge was getting his A. B. degree. But in the day's work at Washington one degree is as useful as the other. Few men ever have had both degrees.

CHAPTER XVIII

MORE ABOUT NATIONAL POLITICS

This story or Western politics, the story of the rise to power of Charles Curtis, the leader of the United States Senate, the President's reliance in every battle with the Democrats, is as large a part of the Coolidge story as it is of the Curtis story. For until one knows the kind of politics with which Coolidge as President has been contending, and must contend, one cannot understand either his victories or his defeats. New England Republican politics are for the most part clean. Western politics, particularly Kansas politics from which Curtis has risen, are clean; they have the New England inheritance, but they are clean in a different way from the rectitude of New England. Kansas more or less typifies a group of Western states which have long controlled the majority in the Republican Party and are conscious of their control. Curtis's rise in Western politics is in many ways deeply antithetical to the rise of Coolidge. But Coolidge ceased to be a New England leader and became a national leader when Harding died in 1923. He has had to deal with Western politics, Western methods, Western men.

182

They have influenced him. And to know what that influence has been and why it came is the reason for this further examination into the career of this Western man who rose in 1923 to such power in the United States Senate.

Early in his congressional career, Congressman Curtis discovered an important fact about the politics of his day; that ward and precinct caucuses were controlled by persons who had the greatest interest in controlling these meetings. Caucuses controlled delegates to county conventions, and county conventions controlled delegates to district and state conventions and they all controlled nominations of political parties. Those, therefore, who controlled caucuses controlled nominations, and those who controlled nominations ruled the land. Congressman Curtis in the mid-nineties found that the rulers of his district were not the rank and file of the people, but those who profited by shaping the trend of politics. In his particular district, control lay with the railroads, the Sante Fe, the Missouri Pacific, and the Rock Island. In Topeka the Santa Fe shopmen and the Santa Fe office people, working with the Rock Island employees, appearing in the party caucuses could control a minority of the Shawnee County convention sufficiently large to dominate it. In Atchison the Missouri Pacific employees held the strategic position. In Horton the Rock Island men dominated. So, being a practical man with a good brain, he went to the sources of control. He made friends with the railroad attorneys who handled this railroad vote. Later, as he came to know his way around in Washington, he made friends with those who controlled the Kansas railroad attorneys, and so became entrenched in power. He was undefeatable in conventions by reason of his accurate knowledge of the forces that dominate men, and at the polls he commanded majorities because of the charm of his personality, and because he had personal relations with all his district. In those days the veterans of the Civil War, organized as the Grand Army of the Republic, held a balance of power in Kansas.

This son of Captain Curtis lavished a genuine affection on the veterans, looked after their pensions, saw that they held the post offices, and gave them his devoted attention. To them he remained "Our Charley" long after the rest of the world had forgotten the sobriquet. With the railroads and the old soldiers back of him he could defy the world in his district. He served the House of Representatives fourteen years, from 1893 to 1907, while Calvin Coolidge was a student, a young lawyer, a town official, a state legislator. How different were these two careers. Coolidge came as from "cool Siloam's shady rill"; Curtis a tawny sunflower nodding in the blighting prairie winds. In Washington Curtis had more patronage than any other Kansas congressman. He had a passion for friendship and he supported it like a prince.

In Kansas, in those days of the first decade of our

century, his enemies charged that Curtis was not a statesman but an errand boy; an errand boy for place-hunters, an errand boy for the railroads, an errand boy for the old soldier who was sadly marching into the sunset. The charge that he contributed nothing to the discussion of public questions in his congressional days was of course capable of rather accurate demonstration. But Curtis had his side. To understand that side is to understand the man who almost next to the President of the United States is, in the midst of the third decade of this century, influencing the political course of our country.

Curtis's mind, like Coolidge's, is factual. But Curtis carried for thirty years in his mind a set of facts about politics entirely different from those in Coolidge's political category. If Curtis had gone to college he would have been a scientist. He never has cared particularly for money. He cares less than Coolidge for theories of life. Jobs please friends, is a simple statement of fact. Friends help in elections, is another simple statement. There was that end, the Kansas end. The Washington end ran thus: Powerful men give jobs to friends. To get patronage be friendly to powerful men. Make friends and serve Kansas; let the reformers go rave. So Curtis became messenger for those who had favors to give. He profited not one penny for himself. He was an honest agent. Speaker Reed early discovered how Curtis could be trusted. Reed used

Curtis. And Curtis became Mercury for Cannon. Cabinet members trusted Curtis. He did not lie; he did not steal; he did not blab. He never stopped working until the job which he had in hand was done, and always it was some one else's job. His commission was slight—just places for his friends. Three times has he been offered a federal judgeship by grateful Presidents, and declined.

Curtis and President Coolidge, starting from unbelievably different bases, have arrived at the same goal. Look at them as they stand together— more or less coequal rulers of the political destinies of this land; antitheses in every unessential point, but affinities in certain complementary differences in that Curtis is affable where Coolidge is grim; Coolidge spare and gaunt where Curtis is pudgy and roly-poly; the President revealing little even by his silence, the senator still more unrevealing in his abundant speech. In his teens the President learned history, economics and sociology from two wise men in college. In his teens Curtis rode the races, saved his money, and more important still, saved his character, and learned from life a bitterer lesson in economics and sociology than Coolidge learned; but just as wise. Out of the New England machine, but never more than a major cog in it, learning politics carefully day by day more by note than by ear, never quite understanding its deeper significance, perhaps probably not comprehending much of its wicked implications, Coolidge came to the highest office in

the land a clean man.   Curtis, making his own
machine as he went from county attorney to the
House of Representatives, from there to the United
States Senate and through the Senate, always the
mainspring of a machine, a machine that ground
through a good deal of mud in its day, knowing
always how dirty it was, yet never profiting by the
commerce in grime, Curtis also came clean to the
highest place in our legislative system.   Each, the
President and the legislative leader, has a New England conscience.   Coolidge's conscience flinches when
business winces, Curtis's when his friends reproach
him.   Coolidge draws and holds a few men by some
mysterious inner quality.   Curtis spends himself on
hundreds, obviously throwing his inexhaustible sup-
ply of affection upon old cronies and new fancies.
Yet in his heart he keeps a sure integrity, a deep
loyalty to the ideals which his life has builded.   A
queer pair this, as alike as two peas within; as different as two stars without!

During the fourteen years in the House, Curtis
had worked with a majority of the men whom he
met when he went to the United States Senate in
1907.   He learned in the House of Representatives
that if he wanted a measure adopted one of the
poorest ways to get it adopted was to introduce it;
one of the best ways was to let a member of a committee that naturally would be in charge of the measure introduce it, then to play upon that member's
vanity, to run errands for that member and other

members of the committee, until he had a majority
of the committee under obligations to Curtis, and
then to steer his godchild through the rapids of
parliamentary procedure until the measure became
a law. His factual mind never went daydreaming.
Always he has had a constructive imagination of a
high order. He knows men as analytical chemists
know their material. He can mix, beat and amal-
gamate men into majorities because he knows their
history, their desires, their weaknesses, their
strength. No other man knows the United States
Senate as Charles Curtis knows it after eighteen
years of intimacy with it.

Senator Henry Cabot Lodge, who preceded Curtis as Senate Republican leader, was a sour man who
enjoyed revenges, being old; and had his pride.
Curtis was Lodge's whip. They said Curtis was
deeply intuitive, that he could tell how a vote was
going upon any measure as an Indian reads the
weather signs. He was not intuitive. He merely
had a lot of facts. He reasoned it all out. He
knew his senators; how they thought, how they
feared, how they fawned and how they voted. He
was no more intuitive than a physicist who mixes
metals and makes amalgams. His intuitions were
not even subconscious processes. They were simple,
logical deductions from a wide array of rather posi-
tive facts about fairly notable men. Few sophisti-
cates infest the Senate. Senators are ordinary two-
legged men who scarcely try to conceal their major

ambitions and rarely succeed in doing so.   Curtis
had been studying them for a quarter of a century
when he got on the Rules Committee of the Senate.
Most of the senators were fellow members of Curtis in the House.   He was a free man in the Senate.
He had won at a primary.   He had to run no
errands in Wall Street in return for his second election.   Nature and his environment made him a conservative.   His friends were conservatives.   His
loyalty held him conservative even if his judgment
ever beckoned him to the liberal side.   But he knew
the liberals, understood each liberal senator's personal equation as well as if he had written its first
statement.

So on the Committee on Rules, Curtis became a
national figure.   For in the Senate measures win or
lose somewhat because senators fear public sentiment, but considerably because senators are horse
traders, swapping votes for each other's minor measures, helping one another in little personal ways.
And the whole ninety-six of them are like little
atoms, each revolving in his own little sphere, larger
or smaller according to the orbit of his mind and
heart, making that insubstantial substance that we
call a legislative body.   And if one man has a master's instinct for horse trading, he can dominate the
Senate and change the color and texture of that
insubstantial thing we call the legislative body somewhat to his own will.   Lodge as leader could not do
it.   Curtis as whip in the Sixty-sixth Congress was

bent more or less to Lodge's will. In the second session of the Sixty-seventh Congress, in the year 1923, Curtis became Chairman of the Committee on Rules, whip of the Senate and actual leader subject only to the whims of Lodge, the nominal leader. But those whims sometimes were disastrous. They affected legislation. Lodge was a New England leader. Little he knew and less he cared what the other man wanted. No horse trader was he. He was a statesman. Large measures interested him. Great policies, the pomp and circumstance of glorious victory were dear to his heart; the acid vinegar of revenge was sweet in his mouth. He played favorites. And Curtis, the whip, had only a little free will. It was in the Sixty-eighth Congress that Curtis became actual and nominal leader of the United States Senate. It was then that he and Calvin Coolidge came into their own high places of power in their own right, by election. How far they had come to meet in that common orbit!

Major issues mean little to Curtis. The very fact that he has been in Congress a third of a century and has sponsored no pet measures of national importance makes it possible for him to take such measures as the gods provide and wrangle them through the Senate much as a herdsman takes his pony out of a herd. Curtis is an instrument in the forces that control movements. He does not inspire movements, is not greatly interested in the whys and

wherefores of causes.   But he does get the day's
work done.   And the thing that moves him is emotional—his old friendships, his deep affections.
Remember that and then consider that this man is in
control of the Republican majority in the United
States Senate.   Now consider three examples of his
power.   Senator Lodge as a leader, a man entirely
interested in foreign affairs, tried for twenty years to
get favorable action on the Cuban treaty.   No one
thought it could be put through the Senate.   It was
one of the first things Curtis, a Senate leader, accom-
plished.   Curtis had one Presidential veto to recon-
cile and the President was sustained, but only by a
majority of one, which we shall consider presently.

But the marvelous thing Curtis did was to close
the Senate without all-night sessions.   For the first
time in forty years this was done because Curtis kept
the calendar clear; kept measures grinding through,
adjourned early, left the senators happy and cleaned
up the slate.   He knew his business; did a workman-
like job, the job of a skilled, conscientious craftsman
in legislations.   Here then we have a powerful man,
motived chiefly by his affections.

Now as to his relations with Coolidge.   In 1924
Curtis's Kansas friends felt that Curtis should have
been on the Republican national ticket as the Vice-
Presidential candidate with Coolidge.   He was a
Western Republican and a regular Republican.
Moreover, his friends presented his name for the

Vice-Presidency. The President's New England friends controlled the convention but they allowed Curtis to be ignominiously snubbed in the convention. The New Englanders did not seriously try to help Curtis. Now to go back to the Presidential vote. When the Senate sustained the President's veto of the Postal Salaries bill under Curtis's leadership, the Senate sustained the veto with one vote—a Democrat under personal obligation to Curtis. A leader who could get one vote to make a majority could have gotten twenty, when the majority was assured. Curtis, knowing how canny the President was, doubtless expected the President to notice this. It proved Curtis a free man. Curtis's loyalty to the President holds, because Curtis is a partisan, but Curtis also is a man before he is a partisan; a man whom Coolidge must study, must consider and sometimes, perhaps, must conciliate.

During his forty years in politics, Senator Curtis has made little money. No political dollar ever stuck to his fingers. He has saved something, but saving was no passion with him as it has been with Coolidge. His economies have been chaste and simple and rather secondary fancies in his life. Probably he will die worth something less than a quarter of a million; a man of no minor vices, no very large virtues if one excepts an eager loyalty to friends without much regard to their worth or standing. Such was the man whom the President of the United States had to rely upon, and the Republican Party

use in formulating the legislative policies of this
country during the first elective term of Calvin
Coolidge. Curtis's life story is peculiarly American.
He was uniquely the product of a democracy, as
Coolidge was, but Curtis was also a Westerner. The
Old West was in his blood, the Wild West, the West
of the Indian, the trader, the cowboy, the booming
West of the eighties, the expanding West which
came under the plow after the Civil War, the restless West which has produced two major political
upheavals in a half century—Populism and Roosevelt insurgency. This West always has been in Curtis's consciousness. He has lived out West all his
life; he has always understood it and to a certain
extent its power for explosion has made him cautious. The power of the West to indulge a certain
reckless joy of life had made him wise. In a party
under the intellectual and political domination of
New England, Curtis was a necessary element for
success. Wherever the conservative administration
has followed Curtis it has minimized its mistakes.
For the West is not New England; in emergency
the West has rarely followed New England. The
West, spiritually, is mated to the South. Curtis,
with his French and Indian blood mingled with that
of New Hampshire and New York, with his childhood and youth spent in the rollicking, lusty environment of a happy-go-lucky people at their play, brings
to leadership in American politics, with all his conservatism, with all his distaste for issues and causes,

a solvent which might in some crisis change the acid of New England to a palatable potion.

But Curtis was but one phase of President Coolidge's Western problem. For nearly twenty years the White House has pondered over another Western puzzle. There was Borah.

CHAPTER XIX

THE DRAGON AT THE GATE

Nine calm months followed the adjournment of
Congress and the recess of the Senate in March,
1925. During those months it became certain that
the President would formally put forth no legislative program. His speeches indicated no new
stirring of his heart. The reporters from day to
day had "the White House attitude" first-hand from
the President. They seemed to feel and they made
it evident to the country that the President was
handling the day's work as the day's work; not as
part of a program, not as a sequence in the presentation of a cause. Prohibition enforcement came up,
a change in the personnel of the enforcing officers
was considered and adopted. The Belgian debt was
adjusted. The railroad problem from day to day
considered; as, for instance, the wisdom of regional
railroad mergers, the justice of increased freight
rates in the West, and the possibility of slightly low-
ered freight rates in the East. The anthracite coal
strike threatened and was casually considered. The
public revenue was discussed and the methods for
raising it. The French debt was considered and cov-

ered with court-plaster. Then slowly it became more
and more certain that "the White House attitude"
which would be the administration program, was
rather definitely in favor of reducing the taxes of
large taxpayers and leaving those of small taxpayers
in statu quo.

As day followed day it became evident that all
this casual consideration of public problems as
labeled the "White House attitude" by the reporters
was not what it seemed. It was, indeed, despite its
casualness, part of a cause, the cause of prosperity,
of property. By certain of his very silences in the
first of the threatened railroad rate increases in the
West, by his attitude toward reducing taxes for the
larger income and inheritance taxpayers, and his
lack of interest in reducing the taxes of the smaller
taxpayers, by his easy acceptance of the inevitable-
ness of the coal strike, it became obvious as the days
and weeks piled into months and seasons that President Coolidge in his own way, quite without dramatic
climax or histrionic effects, yet never shrinking full
responsibility for his position, was outlining a policy
of administration. It was not necessarily nor primarily a legislative policy that he was promoting; but
rather he was giving slant and direction to his entire
administration. The postmaster in the little town
frowned upon the liberals and called them radical.
The judge upon the bench bent his decisions to the
trend of the administration. Administration newspapers became more candid in their editorial expres-

sion about the sacramental character of commerce, about the spiritual beauty of business in general, and in particular they were candid about the blasphemy implied by those who would consider justice before property.

In all this gradual assembling of political and social policy back of the government at Washington, but one major dragon opposed. The dragon at the gate across the pathway of the President's program stood not a man, but the intellectual qualities of a man, the insistent opposition of William Borah, United States senator from Idaho, and chairman of the Senate Committee on Foreign Relations, surely the liberal leader of Congress, if there was any, and leader of all those forces which instinctively oppose and defy the theory of government upon which the Coolidge administration is founded.

It may be well to pause here for a chapter to consider Borah and his battle. As Curtis in the first part of the President's administration became the impersonation of the Republican Party in Congress and the chief reliance of the White House—its rod and its staff, its present help in trouble—so contrariwise may it be said that Borah was the rod of wrath inexorably held before all the implications and aspirations of the Coolidge administration.

Personally, Borah and Coolidge have been on friendly terms ever since Coolidge came to Washington. In the two and one-half years of the Coolidge administration Borah has had easier access and

more frequent entrée to the White House than even
Curtis, the Republican leader. There was much
comradeship and deep respect between the two men,
Coolidge and Borah. Coolidge would have had
Borah on the Republican ticket with him; even
invited Borah at a White House conference to allow
the use of Borah's name on the Republican ticket.
Legend says that Borah responded "at which end,"
and Coolidge took it good-naturedly. Coolidge as
President has been no prima donna, but an adept
politician with a quarter of a century's steady practice behind him, with more years of practical participation in real politics to his credit than any Pres-
dent who has entered the White House for fifty
years. So he would get along with Borah. Borah
has had the patronage from his state. Borah was
not outlawed as La Follette was; was not coldly
scorned by the White House as Norris and Brook-
hart and other Republicans of the left wing were.
Borah stood well politically and personally at the
White House and in Congress. Yet he was the
implacable enemy of everything which President
Coolidge holds dear in his political creed. Borah
and not the Democratic Party, he rather than even
La Follette, who had been winged in his flight before
he fell, was the real opposition to the Coolidge
administration. And Borah came to his leadership
without any organized following, with no propaganda or machine behind what he stood for; indeed,
with no statement of his creed, no platform of his

possible performances, no program for putting his
ideas into reality. Borah for nearly twenty years
has been the incarnation of an idealism which stood
for justice against prosperity. Coolidge vitalized
the belief that without prosperity justice is futile.
The two dramatized the conflict of ideals that
always has raged in American politics. Coolidge
was Hamiltonian; fundamentally and essentially,
Borah was Jeffersonian. Borah, respecting the Constitution, fighting for its implications of justice sav-
agely and without compromise, after all has taken
his political inspiration from the Declaration of
Independence. Coolidge, mystical to the point often
of unreason, had his feet firmly planted in the property protecting clauses of the American Constitution
and his idealism wrapped up in the belief that material progress holds in its processes the guarantees of
justice; that human rights have their best expression
in property right. These two men, Borah and Coolidge, for three years have been fighting whatever
battle there was in American politics that in the first
half of the third decade of the century seemed static
and undisturbed.

Coolidge has depended upon Curtis, the Republican leader of the Senate, and so the leader of Congress, to marshal the regular Republican strength of
Congress against the antagonism of Borah. The
Republicans seemed to have a majority in Congress,
but many times in the past twenty years Borah has
appealed over Congress to public sentiment and has

changed Congress, taken it from Presidents who held
title to it, and so annulled elections and overcome
organizations. This he has done by his sheer intellectual qualities, by his courage and daring. Coolidge has displayed in his career courage enough but
no daring. His courage has been complicated with
caution, and Borah's courage restrained only by his
intelligence.

Borah's name for a decade and more has been
better known than Borah. As a name, his name has
been before the American people for more than
twenty years. It has stood for the brand of goods he
has delivered in Congress; for independence, for far-
sightedness, for loyalty to friends and causes, for a
certain dash of romance that always glamours the
lone fighter, and for a section of opinion in the West
which has come into majorities in government from
time to time and always has hung over majorities
which oppose it like the sword of Damocles. But
Borah, the man, in his senatorial career, has been
little known. He has put on no parades in politics;
never has gone swinging around the circle as a
national candidate. He has appeared fewer times
in the National Republican Convention than any
leader who has been in national politics for two
decades. His face and figure lend themselves gor-
geously to the cartoonist but his picture rarely has
been seen. This has been partly due to modesty,
chiefly due to the fact that personal advertising has
formed no part of his propaganda. He has worked

effectively as his own press agent, his own showman, his own performer and his own cashier.

Physically, Borah always has been restless. On a busy day in the Senate it was his wont to stroll into the chamber, sit for a time listening to debate, move about, stand for a few moments and then go out. In a conference when he could be captured, which was rarely, an hour taxed his patience. Usually he would rise from his chair, pace the room if there was space for him, sit down, look at his watch, remember another appointment, disappear. This was due somewhat to physical reasons, his distaste for cooped-up humanity, but largely to spiritual causes. He has no stomach for compromise. The compromise judgment of a contending group has not interested him. His enthusiasm has been for his own reasoning processes of thought; processes based upon the premise of his own philosophy. His philosophy always has been the complete antithesis of the Coolidgean philosophy. Borah's life passion has been for justice in human relations. Property never has interested him. He has saved little and cared nothing for what he has saved nor for what others have saved. Only as business was honest did he respect its achievements. Time and again in his senatorial career he has shown a deep vitriolic contempt for the large aggregates of business which Coolidge uses with respectful veneration. Borah exposed the sugar trust and Coolidge would have taken the man whom Borah exposed as his Attorney

General. Borah attacked the twelve-hour day in the steel trust and denounced it in a public report as "cruel if not brutal." A Wall Street report declared that Coolidge has invested some of his savings in United States Steel securities. Physically as well as mentally Borah came out of the West; a large man who would be fat if he let himself go, instinctively a hedonist, a good liver, a good fellow with a cleft chin, jowls, and a twinkling eye, a large, expansive, strong but sensitive mouth; the kind of a physical creature who under proper environment might have preferred to play Mercutio into his seventies rather than to be cast for Polonius for one act. It must have been at some sacrifice that he gave up a career as a sybarite for that of a statesman. He came out of the West; out of Illinois through Pennsylvania of old American stock, probably of German origin. His name derives from that of Martin Luther's wife. From the Illinois farm he came alone to the State University of Kansas. There he sat in the seminars of Professor James H. Canfield. With him in the university were gentlemen who afterward attained somewhat more than local fame,—General Frederick Funston, Governor Herbert Hadley, Vernon Kellogg.

From the University of Kansas he went alone to practice law in Lyons, Kansas—in that day a little wind-swept, sun-bleached, weed-bound blister in the prairie where a thousand people saw a great city about to rise. He could not wait for their vision.

Being restless, he went on alone out into the farther West. He had a ticket for Portland, Oregon, but he found a man on the train who spoke well of Boise, Idaho, and again being restless on the train, he got off alone at Boise. There he planted his life and established his career; also quite alone, without influence or friends. He went into politics soon after coming to the state, ran for Congress on the Free Silver Republican ticket, was defeated, but the campaign advertised his law office, and it began to fill up. He married Miss Mamie McConnell, the daughter of a former governor of Idaho, and before Coolidge was admitted to the bar, Borah had become attorney for the great mining and lumbering and timber-owning corporations of the Northwest; corporations which later were to merge into national organizations. Borah served them well. His maturity goes back into another generation. While Coolidge was studying law in Northampton, Borah, appointed special attorney by the governor of Idaho, was prosecuting the labor union leaders who were charged with being responsible for the Cœur d'Alene riots— bloody industrial battles that marked the coming of the metal miners union in the Northwest. In 1903, when Coolidge was city councillor of Northampton, Borah lacked only four votes in the Idaho legislature, which chose the senators in those days, of being sent to the United States Senate. He could have had the four votes if he had tied himself up with certain unpleasant promises. Borah, as lawyer, gave his

legal talent to the great corporations of the Northwest, but he kept his own soul.

In 1907, when Coolidge was in the Massachusetts
legislature, Borah went to the United States Senate.
He had incurred the enmity of organized labor and
got into national fame by prosecuting Big Bill Hay-
wood for the murder of Governor Steunenberg.
Borah also had incurred the enmity of the Hanna
type of conservative Republican in the Northwest
by his open liberalism, his support of what was
then known as the Roosevelt policies. In 1907 certain powerful Republicans in Idaho more or less in
sympathy with the conservative attitude of the
National Republican Committe, had Borah indicted,
charging that he had helped some of his rich timber-
owning clients to evade the law in obtaining land
entries. He was indicted immediately after his election. The local organization prepared for post-
ponements and legal delays that would hold Borah
out of his seat in the Senate for a long time. Borah
sent a friend to Washington to Roosevelt demanding
an immediate trial. Roosevelt, who had no opinion
of Borah's guilt or innocence, sent the word thrilling
down the line from Attorney General to district attorney that Borah must be tried immediately. Borah
was the only witness in his own defense. It took
the jury less than ten minutes to return a verdict to
acquit him. The town of Boise called out the fire
department, rang the church bells, had a militia
parade and Borah had such a triumph as Lentulus

had with returning legions one fine day in Capua.
After that he was the idol of his people. Since the
amendment providing for the popular election of
United States senators, Borah has had no trouble
in returning to the Senate.

Senator Aldrich, the Republican leader of 1907,
misread Borah. The fact that he was attorney for
seven of the greatest corporations of the Northwest was Aldrich's excuse for putting Borah on
the Senate committee on judiciary where he was a
force for militant liberalism for years.

This man, who has been in every detail of his
career the antithesis of Coolidge, is the most powerful opposition to the Coolidge administration. This
opposition, headed by Borah, is the ghost of all that
was not peculiarly personal to Roosevelt in the insurgent movement beginning in 1903 and that is still
alive in 1925. Insurgent progressives, bull moosers,
liberals, all those forces in American politics each
rising out of the other, Borah has led without ever
dramatizing himself as their hero. Roosevelt's progressive leadership began to close in 1914 and another cause attracted him. After 1914 Roosevelt
was staged as an opponent of the Wilson foreign
policy. But in both careers Roosevelt dramatized
himself in his causes. Borah has curiously de-drama-
tized his tremendous interest in the same causes.
Personally, he has been as modest and self-effacing
as Coolidge. Even with his capacity for daring
which Coolidge has lacked, Borah has been sparing

of dramatics. His only political effort has been to return to the Senate. No Presidential candidacy has lured him. He has made no grand gestures for national leadership and probably has never had a party or cult or faction with any sort of permanent organization behind him. Sufficient unto each day has been the issue thereof with Borah. Yet all of his issues have been consistently liberal just as all of Coolidge's Presidential activities, whether in appointment, in the Supreme Court, or a written message, have been consistently intelligent and conservative.

Borah, as chairman of the Senate Committee on Foreign Relations, has had a rather definite foreign policy:

"Over and over again I have said there was no such thing as isolation. Throughout all the debate in the Senate, I have advocated principles of coöperation with other nations when an exigency occurred. I have never opposed coöperation in a grave emergency. What I have opposed from the beginning is any commitment of this nation to a given line of procedure in a future exigency the facts as to which could not be known before the event."

There was probably Borah's foreign policy of fifteen years fairly well boiled down. He voted for the resolution before we entered the war warning American passengers from the ships of belligerents in the war, but he was for the war, yet without enthusiasm. He voted and spoke against the various spy acts during the war and protested against the

Burleson raids upon foreigners in America after the war. He tried with all his might to keep free speech and free assemblage going during the war and probably incurred the enmity of Wilson thereby more than by anything else. For Wilson, once he had entered the war, felt that war itself was a denial of all rights of reasoning because war was force. Borah opposed the ratification of the League of Nations because it committed America in advance as he declared "to a given line of procedure the facts of which could not be known before the event." But more than any other senator Borah was forever hammering upon the front door of the White House for world peace. He hammered through congressional resolutions and congressional debate, and occasional public addresses and newspaper statements. He was responsible for the Arms Conference which Harding called and Hughes engineered. It was his contention in the World Court that we should have international law codified and reëstablished before we have a World Court to adjudicate the law. In these cases he clearly has favored coöperation. He opposed a large army not for reasons of economy, as the Coolidge administration has done, but because of the implications of a large army. Economy as economy never has interested him. Economy as efficiency or economy as an agency to justice appeals to him only as any other agency to efficiency and justice appeals to him, but no more. For the Coolidge sacred cow of economy for the sake of accumulating capital, Borah has no use. He took an active part in opposing the military occupancy of Haiti and San Domingo not as an isolationist, but because he felt the cruel injustice of asking American troops to give their blood to collect bankers' debts and because he realized the tyranny that comes when an army of occupation is set over a feeble people or an inferior race. There was his intellectual mirror in foreign affairs, as revealed by his past senatorial career. It was a man with this record upon whom Coolidge had to rely to promote his foreign policy in the Senate. For we must remember that Borah is a Republican and chairman of the Senate Committee of Foreign Affairs.

Borah must repeat as Coolidge must repeat, as every strong man must repeat, the equation of his life. No bolter he, yet he has been a partisan merely by courtesy. He refused to follow Roosevelt in 1912 out of the Republican Party. He refused to support Taft in the Republican Party. When his party convention in Idaho declared against the direct primary, Borah called the platform a stained glass affair and took the stump in favor of the primary and carried the legislature. When he came up for reëlection the party organization in Idaho marked him for slaughter. He went home, faced the fight manfully, recanted nothing, did not surrender to the organization. In a public speech to his constituents two years before his reëlection, when the primary issue was before the people of the state, Borah declared:

"People have said severe things about me. They say I have never been a Republican; that I have generally been a renegade. Let them be assured that they will not engage me in any personal controversy. The next two years are mine. Only God Almighty can take them away from me, and I shall say what I think, do what I believe right, regardless of the political effect upon myself or any others."

Those words define his spiritual quality; a grave, determined man consistent in his liberalism, militant in his patriotism and, above all, daring in everything, with a certain talent for drama which he rarely uses but which never fails him. Politically he and his kind have been in eclipse for a decade. The minority he leads has been nebulous, unformed. He hardly has led a minority; for half a decade it has been a vague uneasiness in the minds of the various people who produce the Coolidge majority that perhaps something has not been going exactly right. The eclipse of liberalism, which began with our entrance into the war, which grew black in the disillusion that followed the Versailles Treaty, which has been gloomy in cynicism during the procession of corruption under the complacent, high-minded Harding, has been by no means lessened to-day but rather strengthened by the presence of Coolidge in the White House, for Coolidge is honest. He gives the strength of respectability and efficiency to conservative national policy. Under Harding conservatism must have become a short-lived and riotous policy of greed and grab. The Democratic Party during the early years of the Coolidge régime offered nothing in contrast with the conservatism of the administration, no definite liberal policy, no constructive liberal program. The Democratic Party in 1920 was merely calling the Republican Party "another," and making faces rather than issues for the delectation of the public. In the first part of the Coolidge administration, the Democratic Party was not the party of opposition to the President. It is divided upon the issues for which the administration stands. Liberalism and conservatism clash within the Democratic Party; the aristocracy of the Old South and the unwashed Democracy of Tammany make the stamp of conservatism in the Democratic Party even deeper than the Coolidge branch. The liberalism of the Western Democrats and of certain Bryanesque hill-billies and crackers of the South has flaunted a liberalism that approaches demagogy too closely for serious consideration as national policies. The real foe of Coolidge conservatism is Borah's liberalism. Yet the two men personally are self-respecting friends; Borah has beaten a path to the door of the White House under five Presidents, and Coolidge has let no grass grow in the path. Three of these Presidents have been conservatives and the path has been kept hotter in their days than in the days of the liberals. These conservative Presidents have needed to know honestly and without the soft weasel words of courtiers what is in the liberal mind and heart.   This they get from Borah pure and undefiled.   They consulted him, lunched him, dined him, and doubtless, with a sigh for his madness, ignored him, and went on their ways.   It was a sad way for Taft, a bad way for Harding.   As for Coolidge——

PART V

SOME DATA FOR PROPHECY

CHAPTER XX

THE MIND OF CALVIN COOLIDGE

We have now come to a point in the survey of our hero where for a moment we must go back to the five generations of Coolidges who sleep in the little terraced cemetery outside of Plymouth. Three generations of his other ancestors, his mother's people, lie beside the Coolidges. For nearly two hundred years the state of mind that we know as Vermont has bred and inbred itself into Calvin Coolidge with but one outside strain—a remote drop of Indian blood. The marvel of these states of our Union is their difference one from another. Something happens at state lines. What, no one knows. State lines are not altogether topographical, although rivers often make state boundaries and sometimes mountain chains separate commonwealths. Your Vermonter is different from your northern New Yorker and from your New Hampshire man; just as the institutions of the three states carved out of about the same soil, molded in about the same topography, bred in something like the same political institutions, differ from one another. But the difference in the men native to these states is greater than the difference in the externals of the State. Something happens

within state lines that accents all the differences of
the men and all the differences of the institutions.
The constitution of the state of Vermont, an old constitution, has in its preamble something of the folk
wisdom that stamps the Vermonter. The constitution declares that "frequent recurrence to fundamental principles and firm adherence to justice, moderation, temperance, industry and frugality are
absolutely necessary to preserve the blessings of liberty and keep government free." Upon that constitutional preamble the lines of Coolidge's mind have
been gridded in. These lines criss-cross his character, as it were, making the outlines of the puzzle
of his mentality. There they all are—fundamental
principles, justice, moderation, temperance, industry,
frugality. Precious little aspiration, no urge to
adventure, no yearning for larger liberties, no vision
of nobler living. Vermont has no room for these
things, no economic surplus for these things, so no
desire. Vermont stands amid her mountains, a state
of little things, small industries where contented
people have worked at looms by the small-paned
windows where their grandfathers stood; where little Jersey cows in little meadows dot a little land-
scape framed by the little arabesques of the little
hills. No long, straight, challenging lines; no crags,
no cliffs, no awe-inspiring canyons yawn to prod the
imagination of Vermonters. In the list of valuable
articles made in the United States, maple sugar
stands some place below the thousandth item. Ver-

mont proudly boasts that she produces half of the maple sugar made in the world! But her savings account per capita ranks A No. 1. No town is too small to have a savings bank; no home too humble to have a savings account. There is a savings account for practically every house in Vermont. It is the boast of Kansas and Iowa and Nebraska, that there is an automobile and telephone for every house in those states. And alas, they do not boast that there is a mortgage upon at least a third of the houses. The small per cent of mortgages in Vermont is due to two things: first, the thrift of the people; second, the shrewdness of the money lenders. Out of the West, with its broad, muddy, rushing, ugly, ruthless rivers, and its vast mysterious prairies came Lincoln. Out of the Black Hills, stark, strong, ruthless hills, where gaunt, treeless slopes fall at precipitous angles down upon rocky boulder fields, where twisted vegetation at timber lines seems to cry aloud with agony and pain, came Roosevelt; out of the South, with its wide waste lands, its broad, unused rivers, its dark swamps, with its careless, joyous prodigality and vain social caste, came Wilson. Each of these statesmen brought to the White House the impress of his youthful environment and each put the impress of his heart and soul upon his time. So out of Vermont, trim, clean, frugal and fastidious, came Coolidge, tinkering at the times. He will construct nothing. He will mend, patch, gear up and rebuild everything.

"The business of America," quoth Calvin Coolidge, addressing a group of American editors in January, 1925, "is business." Coolidge is a mystic; not a howling dervish like Roosevelt, not an entranced visionary like Wilson, but a dreamer in and of and about material things. "The business of America is business" says it all. Lincoln's whole life was devoted to showing that the business of America is freedom. Roosevelt's life was consecrated to the theory that the business of America is justice. Wilson's one life-long message to the world is, that the business of America is peace. But one can be a mystic, indeed one can be as fanatic as a dervish or a dreamer and still believe in the mysticism which justifies business for its own sake. Coolidge exalts the ideals of the peddler, the horse trader, the captain of industry. He believes that in some occult way, out of their activities will be secreted through the distribution of goods under the beneficence of business ethics and business methods, such justice as mankind needs to grease the wheel of progress. In the same address to the editors, Coolidge said:

"The chief ideal of the American people is idealism. I cannot repeat too often that America is a nation of idealists. That is the only motive to which they ever give any strong and lasting reaction."

In these two statements, that "the business of America is business" and that "the ideal of the American people is idealism" are found the keys

that unlock the chambers of the Coolidge mind; a
mystic faith in the righteousness of a swap. He has
gone through life accumulating little but everlast-
ingly saving. He has touched no tainted dollar in all
his career. Never has a penny that crossed his
palm been smudged. But to save a little every day
has been the ruling passion of his life. On an
income comparatively trivial when contrasted with
the swollen incomes of millions far less able than he,
Coolidge, the lawyer, the legislator, the mayor, the
governor, saved a few dollars every month. He has
made little money and saved much of it. When
Roosevelt came to the White House he told his
friends that he felt it a solemn duty to spend every
nickel of the Presidential salary in the public service. He had a passionate feeling that the salary was
given to him to uphold the social dignity of the
people of the United States, so he entertained like
a prince; kept the White House full of lunchers and
diners. And while it was his temperamental habit
to look as though he had slept in a new suit of
clothes three days after he had ordered it, he dressed
well and patched little. Coolidge, with just as much
patriotic fervor as Roosevelt had, feels that he is
consecrated to the noble ideal of saving every dollar
of his salary that he can that he may set a worthy
example to a wastrel age. So his bank account in
Northampton has grown and grown and he has
invested in American industrial stocks with no sense
of impropriety. The Scotch in Wilson made him

save what he could, but he invested his money chiefly in municipal bonds, state bonds and such securities as would not, under any circumstances, be affected by his Presidential attitude. Yet because Coolidge believes in the power of the esoteric and mystical qualities of business to produce a happy people, he would no more question an industrial investment than he would the bonds of the American Bible Society.

To Vermont, again, one must go for Coolidge's rather definite scorn of passing public opinion. Country life in Vermont or in any sparsely settled mountain country is largely conducted without spectators. Your Vermont farmer continues to exist, not by virtue of any appeal to his fellow man either to persuade him or to please him or to master him, but by struggling with the forces of nature. Consider the story of the Greek cyclops, the descriptions given of the race of cyclops by the sociable, admiration-loving Greek author: "The cyclops are a race living remote from other men, even from each other—shepherds, barbarians—caring not for the opinion of their fellowmen." Evidently those two qualities seem to a Greek identical. They are surely identical in Vermont. Your Vermont has produced no demagogues. Public opinion congeals in the bulb of the Vermont thermometer. It is one of Coolidge's pardonable boasts that he never has changed his mind upon any public question.

But to get back to thrift and investments. Coolidge's investments do not interest the American people whom he represents so perfectly. So long as the people feel as they do feel, so long as by every pragmatic test the theory that the business of America is business works, it is true. The world is what we think it, and out of our thoughts one way or another emerge reality.

After his election in 1924, President Coolidge felt definitely the mandate to reconstruct American government along the lines of his own deep conviction that the business of America is business. Thus one by one the various commissions of government, the Interstate Commerce Commission, the Federal Trade Commission, the Tariff Commission, accepted the dictum of the President that the business of America is business. To protect business, to promote business, to provide for more and better business is the chief aim of every governmental agency in Washington which the President controls. And he is engaging in all this activity for business not stealthily, not with a Puritan sense of sin, but with a high pride, a glowing zeal in his work. He would pursue the thief, the grafter, the camp follower of business as ruthlessly as he would hunt down a destroyer of our institutions. For the oleaginous crew who would stealthily rob the government of any whit of its rights or dues, he would turn as hard and implacable a face as he would to a socialist who sought to change the standard of distribution in industry. He has the fanatic's faith in prosperity as the savior of mankind.

When one understands that faith in a consecrated commerce which shall redeem the world, one may understand why Coolidge would frankly load his Tariff Commission with avowed high-tariff protectionists who feel it their duty to sit, not as unbiased judges upon questions scheduled, but as avowed advocates of protected industries.

Without a high tariff the owners of many of the little mills of New England would either have to close their doors or cut down their capitalization to comport with the physical value of their plant, and either alternative would disturb vested rights, the right of the mill worker to his grandfather's job or the right of a stockholder to his grandfather's dividends. The theoretical right of the millions of consumers to commodities at lower prices would not seem a paramount right when opposed by the definite vested rights of labor or of capital. Coolidge thinks concretely. He takes no chances. His feet are on the ground of a beaten path. He knows his way. He has his faith; he lives up to it. And it has been justified by popular acclaim. He is obeying a mandate.

Those who held opposing views to the President, who held that justice rather than business is our reason for being a country, were appalled at the way Coolidge turned the Federal Trade Commission to

the uses of prosperity. Since King Alfred's day
Anglo-Saxon nations have struggled to protect the
public against restraint of trade. William the Con-
queror added his effort and England made small
headway, for the problem is recondite. A hundred
years after England abandoned her statutes against
forestalling and rerating and engrossing, America
began the task of protecting the public against
restraint of trade. The Sherman Act came and
its interpretation by the Supreme Court in the Standard Oil cases in 1911. For a decade and a half
America, under the Supreme Court decision of 1911,
seemed to have concluded that restraint of trade, if
handled in behalf of the public successfully, should
be surrounded by governmental vigilance which
would in itself affect a partial correction. This public vigilance, which was a part of our anti-trust policy,
would naturally find governmental agencies in a con-
tinuous and intimate society of restraint which promises a means of permanent remedy. Roosevelt
accented publicity as a remedy of restraint. While
he was head of the Progressive movement he prepared and sponsored a bill creating a United States
Trade Commission with this object in view. Wilson
accepted the bill with certain minor amendments and
the Federal Trade Commission was created along
with the supplementary act of the Sherman law.
Publicity was the soul of the commission and its
work. The commission made economic reports
showing trust tendencies and practices. The com-

mission issued legal orders subject to court review
forbidding specified acts of unfair competition.
Under Wilson and Harding the commission, because
of its personnel, was bold in cleaving to the hard
letter of the law which put stress upon publicity of
procedure. Coolidge changed the personnel. He
put in men of his way of thinking. Cases which
formerly had to be held and settled in the open
could, under the new procedure, be settled in conferences that were not public. Publicity withdrew as
an agency in the restraint of trade. Naturally trade
was happy. Business put a handkerchief over the
vigilant eye that was watching it, the eye of publicity.
Then the great national resolution began to wane;
the resolution to get at the heart of the perplexing
thing which seems at times to lead democracy toward
justice and at other times seems to leave democracy
only a choice between socialism and plutocracy, each
equally obnoxious. But President Coolidge, with
all the sincerity of his faith, in business as a civilizing
agent among men, feels deeply that this purpose to
control business in the interests of justice which the
people once had has been revoked by the Coolidge
mandate from the people to safeguard prosperity.

The President's faith in the Divine ordination of
wealth to rule the world and promote civilized progress is evidenced in his opposition to the inheritance
tax. He seems to feel rather deeply that interference with the accumulation of fortunes, however
great, is a wicked perversion of natural law. For

the doctrinaire cult which holds that great fortunes should be disbursed at death, first, to equalize opportunity in a new generation; second, to produce necessary revenue; and third, to eliminate the danger to organized society from vast sums snowballing the wealth of the community in a few hands, Calvin Coolidge has expressed a rather definite scorn. In his speech to the editors in December, 1924, in which he said "the business of America is business," he further declared that he had no faith in Goldsmith's couplet:

"Ill fares the land to hastening ills a prey,
Where wealth accumulates and men decay."

He just does not believe that men decay where wealth accumulates and he said so, contending that the benefits that come from great fortunes through their charitable benevolences offset any evils which might possibly be imagined. His speeches clearly show a deep conviction that in the accumulation of past industry which we call capital lies the intelligent ruling forces of a forward-moving civilization.

Probably this faith in wealth is somewhat due to the fact that he never has had wealth, has viewed it from afar in "wonder, awe and praise"! Witness his preachment upon economy:

"Extravagance lengthens the hours and diminishes the rewards of labor. I favor the policy of economy, not because I wish to save money, but because I wish to save people. . . . Every dollar that we carelessly waste means that their life will be so much the more meager. Every dollar that we prudently save means that their life will be so much the more abundant. Economy is idealism in its most practical form."

If that is not the language of a mystic, when did Emerson or Nietzsche, or Carlyle or Immanuel Kant ever put into one paragraph more faith in their philosophic premises? This is a quality of faith for which men wage war. Any country which might scorn economy, flaunt frugality, punctuality, industry and deny American nationals the royal privileges which come with those virtues, might easily find itself at war with us for denying Americans their rights, with Coolidge in the White House and with his philosophy pushed to its final implication.

When the oil scandal touched his administration, he let two members in his Cabinet resign after long weeks of cold, inexorable inaction in their behalf which became finally translated in their hearts into orders of dismissals. But if we are forced to conclude that political corruption irks rather than arouses him, we must remember that he is a man of small emotional content. He boils at an extremely high temperature. And being congealed, naturally he moves slowly but rather surely to chase the thieves from the sanctuary. He never, however, mistakes the mendacity of the thieves which to him is casual, accidental and sporadic with the business of the holy temple, the accumulation of wealth and its sacred preservation in the hands that hold it. He is more than property-minded. In his creed it would seem that few human rights may not be resolved into property rights. To him how mad must appear the whole era behind him, when men sought to regulate capital, to restrict the activities of capital; when men questioned the wisdom of benevolent plutocracy; the era of reform and reconstruction which closed with the Treaty of Versailles. The leaders of that era made quick exit. Bryan, Roosevelt, Wilson, La Follette passed with their times.

At the end of the era stood three strong Americans. Curtis, leader of the Senate, a Westerner who for thirty years had spent his life buffeting the waves of liberalism, under its various names and phases—Populism, Bryanism, anti-Cannon insurgency, the Rooseveltian Progressives, and the Wilsonian Democracy; Borah, leader of whatever liberalism is manifest at the close of a fifty years' struggle, who like Krishna McCree's dog "has gone a bit of the way with them all"—the Silverites, the Agrarians of the late nineties, the Rooseveltians, even the Wilsonians; and the third of the trio of American leaders is Coolidge, who has never fought for a cause nor against one. Each of the three is equally honest; each has his own kind of courage, entirely sufficient for the needs of his career. By reason of his high office Coolidge should be the leader. But to lead the President must rely upon Curtis and conquer or eliminate Borah. Curtis by reason of his background has no great enthusiasm for the President's program. He will take it, push it, put it through the mill of senatorial routine, but all with little conviction that the program is important. He is imbued with the traditions of the Senate. His first loyalty has been for years to his colleagues in Congress. In a clash with Congress, Curtis in 1923 and 1924 could not be counted heart, mind and soul with the White House.

Borah has never been with the White House nor with the Senate. He has never taken a White House program unless he made it. He can do what neither the President nor Senator Curtis ever has done. Borah can appeal to the electorate. He can make and work with public sentiment. He knows his way to the people.

The era that closed in America with the second election of Woodrow Wilson and in the rest of Christendom closed two years before, left many tag ends of problems to be solved, many crooked lines of advance to be straightened out. It would seem to be the task of any American leader in 1925 to straighten out the dangerous salients of progress which Bryan and the Populists, Roosevelt and the Republicans and Wilson with his Democrats lined out. Coolidge to succeed must mop up; must consolidate the victories of the past three decades, discarding some hopes, abandoning certain advance lines, strengthening others. And to do his work well he must express himself through Senator Curtis, while satisfying Senator Borah and the suspicious minority which generally follows Borah.

In writing historically of a living man, one lacks the climax of finality. This Coolidge drama written in the autumn of 1925 ends in the midst of the first act. Prophecy is the most futile of all man's endeavors. But we may at least collect the data for prophecy.

CHAPTER XXI

THE CHISELING WHITE LIGHT

Only as part of the data for prophecy are we warranted in scrutinizing a President's face. No man can remain the same man that he was after a year in the White House. The white light that beats upon the throne chisels a man's face. If there is vanity there, the chisel finds it and shows it; if there is wickedness in it, complacency, it is all chiseled in. And no man can shield himself from the edge of that chisel. Few men in two and a half years have changed as little as Calvin Coolidge. Yet there has been change. His pictures taken as Vice-President and those taken in the autumn of 1925, show that two years have strengthened his face, but the lines of strength displayed are not lines of radical change. Evidently the man's heart is the same, his convictions are unmoved. The technique with which he attacks problems is best summed up in these lines of his that represent ideals, perhaps, rather than achievement:

"Do the day's work. If it be to protect the rights of the weak, whoever objects, do it. If it be to help a powerful corporation better to serve the people, whatever the opposition, do that. Expect to be called a standpatter, but don't

230

be a standpatter. Expect to be called a demagogue, but don't
be a demagogue. Don't hesitate to be as revolutionary as
science. Don't hesitate to be as reactionary as the multipli-
cation table. Don't expect to build up the weak by pulling
down the strong. Don't hurry to legislate. Give administration a chance to catch up with legislation."

In the governor's office at Boston in 1919, the
President might have paid a little more attention to
"the rights of the weak," and perhaps would a little
less officially be inspired "to help a powerful corporation better to serve the people"; but only a little.
The change that has come into his life has not been
a change of convictions or a change of attitude; the
change has come from an experience, from an appre-
ciation of the deep responsibility of his place, from a
tremendous desire to live up to his opportunity. We
may say honestly enough therefore that the first two
years in the White House hardened the President
if they did not change him. They gave him self-
reliance, cleared off a certain diffidence which seemed
timidity, and a certain unfamiliarity with public men
which made him taciturn. The mid-autumn of 1925
found not a different man, but a stronger man in
the White House than it knew in August, 1923.
This strength of Coolidge was noticed everywhere.
Public men noticed it, particularly reporters noticed
it. His speeches showed it. The speech to the
American Legion in the autumn of 1925 revealed
the President from a new angle. His plea for tol-
erance at home and for international amity and

understanding was almost emotional. His remarks about the economy in the army and navy were all but revolutionary, considering his background. Then quickly followed his speech to the Congregationalists, a plea for spiritual values in a material world. A fine speech, revealing a new man to America. It is this inner quality of Coolidge that always brings him out of the kinks, as men come to know him better. It is this inner quality which makes him ever repeat his career as the inner man is revealed in a situation wherein the outer man comes awkwardly. Then another thing is possible; perhaps the country is getting ready for a spiritual revival, ready to turn to other than material issues and things. If the country is wearying of its golden calf, something prescient in Coolidge would sense the change, something far below his outer consciousness would respond to this movement, and perhaps could lead it; for he seems to be getting ready for a stronger leadership than he has taken in the presidency. There was a certain dropping away of restrictions and qualifications in his utterances and surety in his logical processes, a firm acknowledgment of his philosophical premise that progress depends upon capital, which marked the President for a stronger man than the Vice-President or the governor of Massachusetts. Two years taught him to gauge a stranger better than he could before.

His tremendous majority in 1924 was more or

less of an embarrassment. It was so big that it meant nothing clearly except a protest against radicalism. Coolidge has had to be constructive; but the election gave him a lot of left-handed tools. His face shows a dogged purpose to use effectively whatever the gods have given to him. For instance, take just one job: the American foreign policy and party regularity were hard to combine. Coolidge had a majority in the Committee on Foreign Relations of the United States Senate if he cared to make that majority out of its Democratic members and his Republican adherents. But he could not make a Republican majority. He had to approach his policy only in the spirit of compromise which meant surrender of principles or compromise with party regularity. In his domestic policies he was in something the same position. If New England dominated the Republican Party, it could produce a party majority in Congress. If Coolidge went outside of New England to produce a majority in Congress, he had to accept Democratic support. He came into the White House as he has come into every situation in his life—ignored, snubbed, insignificant. Congress flaunted him in the session of 1923-24. Then slowly he moved along his accustomed cycle into a place of respect and comparative security. All of this slow conquest showed in an undoubtable line of satisfaction that was not pride in the changed face of the President in 1925.

Things move swiftly in the days of radio and airplane, thought transference, sales resistance and mass psychology. This generation of the early twentieth century has done in years what its fathers did in decades and its grandfathers in centuries.

Coolidge has ever been a man set in his way before any given problem. But he has never been a man who could not change his ways quickly when problems changed. A definite quality of mobility also shone in the face of the President that men saw in the autumn of 1925; not an easy mobility, but a want of harshness. He voted with the Rooseveltian Progressives in the Massachusetts legislature and was a mild, non-poisonous variety of Rooseveltian, giving political rather than economic adherence to the Roosevelt faith. If the American people of 1925 should change their ideals in 1928, Calvin Coolidge, who unconsciously takes the protective coloring of his times, might change slowly with them if he repeats himself. He has had, always, to change his exterior in order to repeat. He sloughed off Vermont in Amherst; sloughed off Amherst in Northampton; sloughed off Northampton in Boston. And as the governor who welcomed President Wilson in 1919 with a League of Nations speech, he sloughed off the Massachusetts of 1919 in Washington in 1923. "Our entrance into the League of Nations is a closed episode," he declared in his first message. Then he declared for the World Court which is an adjunct of the League.

Yet for all this want of harshness in his face, for all his mobility, one may see in the face of

Coolidge that the gravest danger which always has hovered over his destiny probably is stubbornness. With all his virtues, he has had inherent in him a lot of determination to have his way. He could change his methods with the hour, but no one has been able to persuade him to give up his ideals for expediency. So have his faults risen out of his virtues. His career since 1920 was not set in dramatic times. The Coolidge who came to Washington in 1920, the Cinderella of his party, was a most undramatic personality. He has never taken strong leadership for economic causes, except in the one major issue of low taxes and government economy.

Now as to his relations with men: he will never be quick at judgments of men, but he is speeding up. He has changed the White House force that surrounds him somewhat, and has impressed every one about him with his own Vermont notions of thrift and frugality in terms of time. He desires subordinates who step lively, who are brief, who are exact, who are punctual. Sometimes he is cross with those who do not reckon time in terms of money. The unpunctual servant to him is a waster. The President knows what each White House official minute means in terms of dollars and he is visibly annoyed at the prodigality of those who serve casually. He may snap at them, but it is not that he is unkind. There is no meanness in that serene and placid eye. He is, when he cracks the sharp whip of his Yankee annoyance at a secretary who lags or interferes with the day's routine, as impersonal as a crosscut saw and just as merciless, but he is also justified by his faith. No vagrant, personal whim or pique inspires his petulance. It comes from the abiding conviction of his heart that money is potential wealth, that wealth may become capital, that capital is the seed of progress and progress the salvation of man.

He has no spare time. When he is not actually conferring with men, giving orders to his subordinates, discussing problems, writing speeches, orders or opinions, he is cogitating. He has no idle time for expansive inanities. If he sits at a public banquet, abstracted, looking like a man who had just encountered a bad smell, he is preoccupied, considering something remote from the scene, trying to give the people of the United States value received for the salary which they pay him. His silence is somewhat the by-product of his faith, a part of his program of economy, an essential of his character. With Coolidge, nothing comes easy and goes easy. The waste of time and energy, for instance, which Congress spent in considering and rejecting the nomination of Charles Warren whom the President desired as his Attorney General put Coolidge's temper upon a raw edge. But overnight his common sense told him that it would cost more to fight than it would to surrender and he surrendered with the appointment of Sargent. Generally President Coolidge's emotions have as their basis some cash-register explanation which is perhaps an obvious paradox to those who do not comprehend his faith nor understand the mechanical processes of his logical mind working from its premise that in economy is the soul and seed of progress; that out of waste and extravagance came the fall of man.

Now after the World War, this was the American attitude—this belief in the sacrosanct quality of business in life. From time to time in American history the business conscience has been our guide. The average American state moves with the tides of feeling from one extreme to another in considering the value of the dollar. The almighty dollar fluctuates in its place in the American esteem. American politics register the fluctuation. We have at times produced national leaders as the result of the disturbances of our politics, who held in withering contempt the whole dollar cult of their adversaries. These waves of revulsion against the dollar deity have landed Jefferson, Jackson, Lincoln, Roosevelt and Wilson in the White House. The receding waves have given us Washington, Hamilton, the Adamses, Pierce, Taft and Coolidge. But in all those waves of feeling one state has stood staunch. Vermont has followed no leader who trifled with business, who put human liberty above a stable commerce. Vermont was one of two American states in 1912, when the waves of altruistic emotion dashed high, that voted for Taft. Vermont never flinches. It is the "great rock in a weary land."

CHAPTER XXII

BACK TO VERMONT

And it all comes back to Vermont. "Vermont," said Coolidge, "is my birthright. My folks are happy and contented. They belong to themselves, live within their income and fear no man."

To appraise Calvin Coolidge we must never forget that Vermont has preserved perfectly the fundamentals of American life, " firm adherence to justice, moderation, temperance, industry and frugality," and thereby has preserved with remarkable fidelity "the blessings of liberty and a free government." But we must also understand that Vermont has preserved these things in isolation, harking back to a day that has passed in America. The fields and the factories of Vermont lie alongside each other. Men go to the fields and the children to the factories, and their children go to the fields and their fathers to the factories, making a full-time, diligent year. They live near the economic margin without want. Good-looking farm and village houses that would cost from eight to twenty-five thousand dollars to-day, houses built on straight colonial lines, houses built by straight colonial ancestors adorn the fields

238

and villages, surround the little factories. In these simple, beautiful houses the meager descendants of the large families of another day rattle around almost audibly, and Europeans traveling through Vermont, seeing a well-housed, well-clad people, ask: "Where are the peasants?" The peasant is as far from the cosmos of Vermont as the industrial worker of Lowell, Lawrence and Fall River, Massachusetts, is from the hereditary factory worker in the little whirring mills of Vermont. Indeed, the peasant is as far from Vermont as the Vermont farmer on his piddling ten or fifteen acres of arable land, mowing his grass lot with a safety razor, garnering his crop in one barn loft, is removed from the Missouri Valley farmer, who is less prosperous in fact but more addicted to visions of grandeur with his acres numbered by the hundreds and his mortgage accounted by the ten thousands. And all of them, the Vermont farmers, the Vermont factory hands, are as far removed from the sinister influences of capital which cloud and depress the industrial workers of Pennsylvania, West Virginia and the Middle States above the Ohio, as the abandoned forges and foundries of the Vermont farmer are from the United States Steel plant to-day. Save and work, work and save, will produce salvation in Vermont. They will not always produce salvation in Kansas nor Michigan nor California.

To understand Coolidge we must first of all give him credit for a clean, hard-fibered brain, for an absolutely honest heart, for a noble soul. His limitations are in his experiences. He told a Kansas girl that he had never ridden in a Pullman car until he was nominated for Vice-President. Enter the house in which he was inaugurated; a decent house, a house of an honest, self-respecting, law-abiding, God-fearing father and grandfather; a house of public servants for three generations, men who have served as selectmen, constables, deputy sheriffs for a hundred years. The room where Coolidge took the oath of office has every necessary and useful piece of furniture for living a civilized life. But in the little square room not over sixteen by sixteen, with the plain rug in the center of the unpainted floor, with the bookcase-secretary dating back to the eighteen sixties in which are law books, two dictionaries, a doctor book, and account books piled on two shelves, there is not one hint of beauty, of luxury, of the expansive joy that men of other American sections get in the adornments of life, if one excepts in the Coolidge home the geranium potted and canned in the rectangular bay window that enlarges the simple room by a few square feet. On the plain nondescript table is a guest book. Beside the ink bottle lies a pen. Col. John Coolidge will tell the visitor to sit in the solid, modern, fumed oak dining-room chair that stands beside the desk and will instruct the visitor to sign the guest book. Then he will say:

"If you use that pen you will use the one the

Copyright by Underwood & Underwood

THE COOLIDGE HOME IN PLYMOUTH

"Enter the house in which he was inaugurated; a decent house, a house of an honest, self-respecting, law-abiding, God-fearing father and grandfather."

(Page 240)

President used to sign the oath of office when he was sworn in."

Observe the pen! a thin, pearl-handled pen, slimmer than a pipestem, tapering at one end and with a gold ferule at the other in which the pen sticks. Such a pen has not been seen on land or sea for a generation outside of Vermont. To a visitor's question about the pen, Col. Coolidge will answer:

"Let me see; we have had it something more than fifty years."

There is the story: careful, conscious, saving. There stands Vermont! The house where Coolidge was born lies in a little village surrounded by the lovely hills. Three houses are nested like three white eggs in a green bower. In the attic of one of the three houses of the village of Plymouth may be found a lot of farm and household tools carefully saved, put away against Heaven knows what emergency for four generations; the hand loom, the carding comb, the spinning wheel, all the homely, ugly, useful things that our forefathers used in wrestling with a stern environment for life. There they are saved and not kept. A vast difference lies between those two words. In the South things are kept in the attic; kept in fond recollection, for deeply sentimental reasons with no thought for their future use, with little thought of their past necessity; kept because they are hallowed by old memories; kept because they reflect the grandeur of another day. But the trinkets and tools in the Coolidge attic are saved;

saved for use in some future emergency; saved because to the Vermonter waste is suicide. When Governor W. W. Stickney, of Vermont, nominated Coolidge for President in 1924, the climax and close of his three-minute speech declared that the President in a marked degree exemplified the Vermont family characteristics, "that they never wasted any time, they never wasted any words, and they never wasted any public money."

A picture of a Vermont legislature shows two hundred or more typical Vermonters, with not one fat man; all spare, gaunt, trim, neat, handsome men who have never wasted time at meals nor calories in their food. Coolidge is from the heart of that group, an "over-the-mountains man." It was said fifty years ago that you could always tell an over-the-mountains man because he carried an ox goad and wore a smock. Oxen are not uncommon in the streets of Ludlow. Coolidge as mayor, as senator, as lieutenant governor, as governor, as Vice-President, going back to Plymouth, Vermont, to help his father with the summer work, often wore his shirt outside his trousers. His pictures show him thus wearing the peasant's smock but with the landlord's dignity and distinction. The town of Plymouth has fewer people than it had before the Civil War, about as many as were there during the Revolutionary War. Among his classmates in the academy, not one remained in Ludlow. The class picture which showed his day of pride turned up in

COOLIDGE HELPING GRANDFATHER COOLIDGE

"Coolidge is an 'over-the-mountains' man; because he carries an ox goad and wears a smock."

(Page 242)

Reno, Nevada, but no Coolidge ever has gone West. He has remained there mind and soul and heart, a simple man bred of a simple people. During the days of his rise he went back to Ludlow to make a speech at the Ludlow Academy and it was as good a speech as he ever made. He shirks nothing, forgets nothing, asks little of life.

Across from his father's house is the little wooden church with the varnished pine ceiling and walls beautifully matched in inch and a half boards, the substantial, hard-wood pews decently carved, the pulpit unadorned and dignified; a union church where men of all creeds worship the God of their fathers. Your Vermont mountaineer is not pious, never sanctimonious nor given to creedal wrangles, but he is deeply religious, deeply conscious of a power outside himself that makes for righteousness. From this union church and Sunday School, without creedal or factional dissension, the boy, Calvin, took the faith of the Puritans, the passionate belief in the nobility of man and the goodness of God. Here the mystic was born. With no other exterior aids was his faith implanted, but it goes deep into his heart. And because he believes in the goodness of the things which his childhood and youth saw so unmistakably —the worth of industry, the value of frugality, the high honor of capital, the decent attitude of labor, the compact organization of a simple society in neighborly affection—his faith has flooded into his whole life. No part of his being or thinking or feeling is untouched by this mystic faith that civilization as a going concern depends upon the preservation of a healthy commerce.

One day in the White House the reporters asked the President why he always had rich men and politicians about him; why he did not invite to the White House representatives of the arts—painters, sculptors, poets.

"What poets?" asked the President.

They were listed for him, Vachel Lindsay, Amy Lowell, Carl Sandburg, Louis Untermeyer, Edna St. Vincent Millay, Edwin Robinson, and the rest. He paused a minute, reflected and drawled meditatively:

"When I was in college a man by the name of Smith used to write some verse."

And the episode closed. The question did not touch his interest. The arts are, doubtless, good things in his world but extraneous, unimportant. They are not in his faith necessary components of an orderly and useful life. Vermont has produced no more artists than Kansas. Next to Coolidge, the greatest man who ever came from Vermont was Admiral Dewey, who started a war with the laconic phrase: "You may fire when you are ready, Gridley!" No more fuss and feathers than just that! Whereupon the United States became an empire. It is the Vermont way. Going back to Vermont this is what we get.

But is Vermont enough? This is a big country

in which are many minds and many ways of life. That Vermont epitomized the caste of thought at the end of the first quarter of a century in America no one seriously can deny. Calvin Coolidge is the man of the hour. But the sands run swiftly in the hourglass. Thrift, frugality, punctuality, precision—the business virtues—may not always suffice.

Here in this story we have set down something of the man, of his background, of his vision and of the deep tides of politics that have drawn him into a place of power. These currents from the strong, homely well-springs out of the heart of rural New England may lose control of American life. Vermont—staunch as she is, often is alone in her simplicity—indeed during the last half century Vermont generally has been out of sympathy with the passing moods of America. Coolidge's life has had in it little drama; because he has faced little opposition. His progress has been with the stream of tendencies in American life. Never has he breasted it. While he rides the wave, his course will maintain its calm. But if the wave spends its strength, then— perhaps the rocks, the crash, the wreck.

But that figure encroaches upon futile prophecy.

CHAPTER XXIII

WHAT IT ALL MEANS

The strongest currents of politics are in the undertow, submerged currents that scarcely reach our upper consciousness. America chose Coolidge and stood by him not for what he was on the surface but for what he was and what Americans were beneath the surface. They feared change. He was cautious. Deeply they distrusted adventure, and beneath partisanship and the clamor of the campaign of 1924 Americans believed in business as the savior of the times. They did not vote for Coolidge for what he had shown them in the White House. He proved himself an ineffectual leader. Congress defeated him time and again, defied him; more or less insulted him and he was powerless. But the voters returned the Congress which thwarted and humiliated the President and by comparably the same majority by which they returned the President. The struggle between Coolidge and his Congress was in the upper and visible spheres. In the undercurrents of life, in the submerged part of the great iceberg that is Coolidge, he was caught by the popular cur-

rent. In that undercurrent his mysticism, his simplicity, his dignity, even the limitations of his faith,
touched the popular mind. People forgot the obvious but unimportant faults that rose into the line of
vision. It was not that they voted for a superman. It
was not that propaganda swung them off their feet.
But the real Coolidge, the Coolidge born of three
New England generations of public servants, the
Coolidge who had twenty times gone before the people and nineteen times had won, the Coolidge bred
out of the Vermont constitution, recurring to fundamental principles, adhering to "justice, moderation,
temperance, industry and frugality," that invisible
Coolidge that was more real to America than the
visible Coolidge. Surely that gaunt, taciturn Yankee
who quacks when he talks, that tactless, cheerless
creature of a doleful and disinheriting countenance,
who rode to his inauguration with his smiling wife
and his complacent Republican Senate leader both
beaming with pardonable pride and exemplary joy
while he looked like a mummer on a hearse—that
Coolidge did not win the election. The people chose
another and better man! The deeper, stronger currents of politics are submerged.

With the ascension of Calvin Coolidge to the
Presidency came also his kind to leadership all over
America. The whole country since 1920 has been
flooded with replicas of the Coolidgean type. Governor's chairs are warmed by stern, masterful, pa-
tient men who believe in the divine right of capital

to rule the various commonwealths. Mayors, district attorneys, constables all reflect the mood of the hour. In another day the land was noisy with the rush and clamor of ten thousand little Roosevelts, and a myriad of miniature Wilsons hurrying about establishing justice and putting capital in its proper place in the scheme of things. They were not imitators. They came before Roosevelt and Wilson. If any one was an imitator, it was the greater leader of the day.

Moreover the issues in every American state in the early nineteenth century were practically the issues at Washington. The state or city that did not adopt a budget system was poky beyond words. Tax reduction has been for half a decade a city, county and state-wide slogan. It came from the popular heart. Twenty years before other issues came out of the heart of the people. In the first decade of the new century, issues of social welfare, broadening democracy and business morality were hot in the political pot. In those days which made Roosevelt, states were adopting woman suffrage, prohibition, the initiative and referendum, were regulating the hours and service of women, were evading the Constitution by directly electing United States senators and demanding income and inheritance taxes. It was another and a different day.

But America was not isolated—even then Lloyd George was leading in England. The socialists were rising to power in Germany. Men like Nitti were

in control in Italy, and Jaures, the socialist and paci-
fist, was the outstanding figure of France. The
deep undercurrents of politics ran freely across the
world. These currents made the leaders of that
day.

The one thing world leaders had in common in
1910, was a cheerful faith, a readiness to adventure
into new political fields, an open mind upon all
social vistas. Christendom at the beginning of the
new century was a world of hope. The under-
currents, the widespread and powerful forces that
moved men to see a vision of a new world, moved
them to choose leaders after their own hearts. The
hope of the world chose its leaders. In that hope
for a better time was a willingness to change the
established order. More important than the hope
and intention, was an ardent popular trust in the
instinctive common intelligence of humanity to work
out some nearer approach to justice in human relations than social custom and political formulæ gov-
erning at that time guaranteed. The world in those
decades that ended with 1914 moved in a cycle of
hope.

In 1925 mankind in the west had changed completely the leadership of the world. Men were backing
Hindenburg, Mussolini, Baldwin, Dawes, Coolidge,
not because any more than the leaders whom the
electorate backed in another day, these moderns had
great wisdom, exceptional personal charm, moving
eloquence, or powers of political persuasion. The

world in the 1920's backed its leaders as it always chose them; to conform to the visions in its heart.

The heart of the world in the midst of the third decade of the twentieth century was cold with fear. For in the first upheaval of the World War men saw dreadful things. At the same time they aspired madly under the stir of propaganda which they accepted for a moment in their war intoxication. Their aspiration, the climax of two decades of idealism in world politics, was the vision of a new world. As the new world loomed nearer, when war ceased, those who were responsible for the governments of the earth, whether sitting in parliaments, or in banks, or at military desks, or in executive offices, felt tremors under them, feared displacement of the old order, foresaw the fall and chaos of many useful institutions. Also they saw in the war the brutality, the selfishness, the lusts and greeds of men all unleashed. So, aghast at many horrors—horrors past, horrors present, and horrors future, the leadership of the modern world stood paralyzed. Their fear spread. Bolshevism arose in Russia. It gave carnate substance and form to the dread that was inspiring the sick timidity creeping over civilization. Bolshevism became the necessary devil with which to conjure the fears of mankind.

So all over the white man's earth, people at the close of the first quarter of the new century were clinging to their dream of the old world; the world that was before 1914—a solid, substantial, orderly,

workable, material world, in which the approximate
of justice was not so low but that reasonably
righteous men could satisfy their souls with it.

Meanwhile, into these new modern times, when
all the world is clinging to the old order with terror
in its heart, a new element of justice has come. Industry by its mass production of material things,
turning them out of the factory by millions, has distributed through the ordinary agencies of a rather
sordid commerce, mountains of material things
springing in myriads from the machines; distributed
them with no puling thought of justice, but only
because the mountains could not pile up at the factory doors. These things—needs, comforts,
luxuries, houses, clothes, food, fuel, motor cars,
radio sets, telephones, tooth paste, floor coverings,
electric household machines, labor-saving farm tools,
cement highways, tall buildings, public halls, dry
goods and fancy groceries—have been spread out
among all the peoples somewhat equitably. We
have made, despite the reactionary character and
quality of our politics, through the commercial mo-
mentum of the whirring wheels, a kind of justice
in the distribution of this world's goods; an equitable
distribution which laws and political forms and cus-
toms would have denied to us under the reign of
terror in our hearts. The fountain of justice
blocked at its political source has gushed forth in an
unexpected vent. The mysticism of Coolidge and
the leaders of his day, their faith in the occult power

of mere business to produce justice, is thus somewhat justified. Baal has made the waters spring from the rocks of his altar.

So Calvin Coolidge, sitting tight with the other world rulers of his caste and kind, sitting tight along with a wilderness of Coolidges in miniature over the land, Coolidge, differing only from his European contemporaries as national temperaments produce slightly different variants of a common type, Coolidge, Heaven sent out of the fear in our own hearts, rules us after the ways of our own desires; a political god created in our own image. Here is democracy functioning even in a land which at the moment would like to be a plutocracy. What more terrible spectacle of the inexorable power of democracy has man ever produced than this: the power of democracy that triumphs in the very sanctuary of its enemies and guffaws even their victory to scorn. Surely a world which can pick so nicely, men perfectly fashioned after its own desires, need fear no tyrants when its mood shall change.

The apparent and conspicuous Coolidge seen with a naked eye is an enigma. But the real Coolidge who went in a straight though not strong but always graceful line from Plymouth to the White House, surely was no accident. The more one knows of his inner depths and of the secret places of the heart of America, the surer one becomes that Calvin Coolidge's career was inevitable, his star invariable, his success the natural course of things.

Redwood Library

SELECTIONS FROM THE RULES

1. Three volumes may be taken at a time and only three on one share. Two unbound numbers of a monthly and three numbers of a weekly publication are counted as a volume.

2. Books other than 7-day and 14-day ones may be kept out 28 days. **Books cannot be renewed or transferred.**

3. Books overdue are subject to a fine of one cent a day for fourteen days, **and five cents a day for each day thereafter.**

4. Neglect to pay the fine will debar from the use of the Library.

5. No book is to be lent out of the house of the person to whom it is charged.

6. Any person who shall soil (deface) or damage or lose a book belonging to the Library shall be liable to such fine as the Directors may impose; or shall pay the value of the book or of the set, if it be a part of a set, as the Directors may elect. All scribbling or any marking or writing whatever, folding or turning down the leaves, as well as cutting or tearing any matter from a book belonging to the Library, will be considered defacement and damage.